Study Guide and Workbook

Cultural Anthropology
The Human Challenge

TWELFTH EDITION

William A. Haviland
Professor Emeritus, University of Vermont

Harald E. L. Prins
Kansas State University

Dana Walrath
University of Vermont

Bunny McBride
Kansas State University

Prepared by

Marjorie M. Snipes
University of West Georgia

THOMSON
WADSWORTH

Australia • Brazil • Canada • Mexico • Singapore • Spain • United Kingdom • United States

ISBN-13: 978-0-495-38199-0
ISBN-10: 0-495-38199-3

Thomson Higher Education
10 Davis Drive
Belmont, CA 94002-3098
USA

Contents

Introduction:

Why Should You Use the *Study Guide* and *Workbook*?

Your instructor may or may not require the use of this study guide and workbook to accompany William Haviland's textbook, *Cultural Anthropology: The Human Challenge,* Twelfth Edition. However, there are some important reasons why you might find it helpful as you begin your study of anthropology.

First, using a study guide and workbook along with the main textbook for the course forces you to simply spend time with the material. You have probably found that when you think you have read an assignment for a course, often you actually can't recall much of what you read. By adding time to your reading for answering review questions, going over key vocabulary, and so on, you fix the information in your memory in a far more thorough manner. The time you spend each day on your study guide and workbook will help you to spend less time "cramming" for exams later on.

Second, putting things in your own words, as the study guide and workbook requires, is the best way to make the subject your own. Education researchers agree that this is a good way to ensure that simple memorization is replaced by true comprehension of information. In addition, the exercises which encourage you to grasp concepts rather than memorize words will help you on tests, where your instructor may phrase things in different ways than your textbook author does. This workbook also offers you the opportunity to construct charts which will help you in studying, to do exercises based on maps and diagrams that can visually fix the material in your mind, and to apply anthropological methods to various real life problems. Make the book your own; write in it; do the exercises you find useful and skip the ones you don't. This guide was prepared to help you.

Each chapter of the Study Guide and Workbook contains several sections. A *synopsis* of the chapter is followed by an outline of *what you should learn from the chapter.* Then there is a section of *key terms and names* for you to define or identify and a list of *review questions* which can be answered in a few sentences. There is also a *fill-in-the-blank* section to help you review. In addition to *exercises* which range from the very difficult to the playful, there are *multiple-choice practice questions, true/false practice questions, practice matching sets, short answer questions,* and *practice essays.* These are excellent ways of preparing for the various kinds of examinations your instructor may prepare. Your instructor may also choose to use parts of this study guide for homework or extra credit assignments. If used conscientiously this book will be a helpful complement to your textbook.

Marjorie M. Snipes
University of West Georgia

Chapter 1

The Essence of Anthropology

Synopsis

Challenge Issues: What is anthropology? How do anthropologists do what they do? How does anthropology compare to other disciplines? This chapter introduces the discipline of anthropology as the study of humankind and challenges us to consider the astounding degree of adaptation that humanity has made over time and place. There are four major fields/subdisciplines of anthropology: physical anthropology, cultural anthropology, archaeology, and linguistics. Each of these seeks to produce useful generalizations about people and their behavior, to arrive at the fullest possible understanding of human diversity, and to understand those things that all human beings have in common. Using examples such as the cultural differences related to human organ transplant, infant sleeping patterns, traditional healers versus modern medical practitioners, and the excavation and analysis of recent skeletal remains to investigate human rights abuses, this chapter makes the practice of anthropology extremely relevant in today's increasingly globalized world.

Chapter Objectives

    I.   the development of anthropology

   II.   the anthropological perspective

  III.   anthropology and its fields

  IV.   anthropology, science and the humanities

   V.   anthropology's comparative method

  VI.   ethics

VIII.   anthropology and globalization

Key Terms

anthropology
applied anthropology
archaeology
biocultural
comparative approach
cultural anthropology
cultural resource management
culture
culture-bound
empirical
ethnography
ethnology

fieldwork
forensic anthropology
globalization
holistic perspective
hypothesis
linguistic anthropology
molecular anthropology
paleoanthropology
participant observation
physical anthropology
primatology
theory

Exercises

The Anthropology Resource Center (ARC)

The Anthropology Resource Center is a dynamic, subfield-specific website that provides a wealth of materials for both students and instructors to reinforce key concepts in anthropology. All of the resources and activities encourage students to apply anthropology beyond the textbook and classroom. ARC can be reached through the weblink http://thomsonedu.com/. After selecting the discipline of "Anthropology" under "Humanities and Social Sciences," go directly to ARC for a wide range of resources that bring anthropology to life through pictures, interviews, news items, interactive displays, maps, and more. (This site is passcode-protected for both instructors and students.)

Review Questions

1. What are the four subdiscplines (or fields) of anthropology? How are they related to each other?

2. In their research, how do anthropologists attempt to be as objective and free from cultural bias as possible?

3. Distinguish between ethnology and ethnography.

4. Explain in what sense anthropology is a relatively recent product of Western civilization.

5. How does anthropology use the research of many other disciplines?

6. What is a holistic perspective and why is it important to anthropology?

7. Cultural adaptation, development, and evolution are three general concerns of anthropologists. How are they interrelated?

8. Why do archaeologists excavate sites from a historical period when many documents provide information on recent culture?

9. What is the significance of "The Garbage Project?"

10. Who are Franz Boas and Matilda Coxe Stevenson?

11. With what aspects of language are linguists concerned?

12. Discuss why anthropology is considered the "most liberating of all sciences."

13. Distinguish between the social sciences and the humanities.

14. Discuss how human behavior and biology are inextricably intertwined. Provide examples.

15. Explain why it took so long for a systematic discipline of anthropology to appear.

16. Explain how the work of an anthropological linguist can contribute to our understanding of the human past.

17. Discuss the problems inherent in the science of anthropology.

18. Discuss the ethical problems that could arise in the process of anthropological research.

19. Why are Japanese reluctant to give and receive organ transplants?

20. Describe the role of the ethnologist, giving an example of the sort of study an ethnologist would produce.

21. What is participant-observation? What are its advantages and disadvantages when compared to other social science methods?

22. Why might it be advisable to do research outside one's own culture prior to studying one's own?

23. What is meant by cross-cultural comparison? What significance does it have?

24. What is significant about the involvement of traditional healers in the fight against HIV/AIDS in South Africa?

25. What is the importance of fieldwork in the subdisciplines of anthropology?

26. What is globalization and why is it increasingly important today?

27. How does anthropology distinguish between a "nation" and a "state"?

28. What is the role of applied anthropology in addressing cross-cultural health issues around the world?

29. What is the difference between a hypothesis and a theory?

30. What might be accomplished by research into one particular culture?

31. What distinguishes anthropology from the "hard sciences?"

32. Why must anthropologists exercise caution prior to publishing the results of their research?

33. To whom are anthropologists ultimately responsible?

34. What is the role of imagination in the development of science?

35. What are the dangers of culture-bound theories?

Fill-in-the-Blank

1. Anthropology is the study of _____ everywhere, throughout time.
2. Over the last _____ years anthropology has emerged as a tradition of scientific inquiry.
3. Anthropologists recognize that human behavior has both _____ and social/cultural aspects.
4. Anthropology is divided into four fields: _____, _____, _____, and _____.
5. An example of a practical application of physical anthropology is _____ anthropology, in which anthropologists testify in legal situations concerning human skeletal remains.
6. Archaeology is the study of culture based on _____ remains.

7. An in-depth description of a specific culture is called a[n] _____.

8. Comparisons of "housework" shows that _____ spend less time on household tasks than Westerners do with all their time-saving gadgets.

9. A tentative explanation of the relation between certain phenomena (e.g., "The light failed to work because the filament was broken") is called a[n] _____.

10. The ethnographic method is commonly referred to as _____.

11. Cultural resource management is a branch of _____.

12. Anthropology demonstrates that there is no _____ basis for the notion of human races.

13. The physical anthropologist applies all the techniques of modern _____ to achieve fuller understanding of human variation and the ways in which it relates to the different environments in which people lived.

14. Today, _____, or the anthropological study of genes and genetic relationships, is another vital component of biological anthropology.

15. The term _____ refers to worldwide interconnectedness, signified by global movements of natural resources, trade goods, human labor, finance capital, information, and infectious diseases.

16. Socially organized bodies of people with a common understanding of their ethnicity are referred to as _____.

Multiple-Choice Practice Questions

1. Anthropology is _____.
   a. the study of Western culture primarily through the analysis of its folklore
   b. the study of humankind everywhere, throughout time
   c. the study of nonhuman primates through behavioral analysis
   d. the study of the species Homo sapiens by analyzing its biological but not its cultural dimensions
   e. the analysis of humankind from the subjective perspective of one group

2. The systematic study of humans as biological organisms is known as _____.
   a. linguistic anthropology
   b. cultural ecology
   c. cultural anthropology
   d. archaeology
   e. none of these

3. Anthropology differs from other disciplines that study humans in its use of _____.
   a. cross-cultural perspective
   b. evolutionary perspective
   c. holistic perspective
   d. comparative method
   e. all of these

4. Which of the following is not a field of anthropology?
   a. cultural anthropology
   b. genetics
   c. archaeology
   d. physical anthropology
   e. linguistics

5. As part of your job, you may study the frequency of blood types in human populations, watch the behavior of monkeys and apes, or dig for early hominid bones from East Africa. You are a/an _____.
   a. entymologist
   b. primatologist
   c. ethnologist
   d. physical anthropologist
   e. cultural anthropologist

6. Theories about the world and reality based on the assumptions and values of one's own culture are_____.
   a. simplistic
   b. irrational
   c. culture-bound.
   d. relativistic
   e. inductive

7. An archaeologist might attempt to _____.
   a. study material remains to reconstruct past cultures
   b. study present languages to reconstruct when they diverged from a parent stock
   c. study garbage to explain contemporary behavior
   d. "study material remains to reconstruct past cultures," "study present languages to reconstruct when they diverged from a parent stock," and "study garbage to explain contemporary behavior"
   e. "study material remains to reconstruct past cultures" and "study garbage to explain contemporary behavior"

8. An archaeologist studies_____.
   a. potsherds
   b. paleoecology
   c. genetic drift
   d. garbage
   e. potsherds, paleoecology and garbage

9. _____ is that branch of anthropology concerned with humans as biological organisms.
   a. Archaeology
   b. Cultural anthropology

    c. Ethnology

    d. Physical anthropology

    e. Paleontology

10. The focus of anthropology is on both evolution and culture as such it is able _____.

    a. to address the "nature versus nurture" question

    b. to address certain ethical issues

    c. to discuss the efficacy of various research methods

    d. to address the qualitative vs. quantitative methods issue

    e. to address the political questions of the day

11. In-depth descriptive studies of specific cultures are called _____.

    a. ethnologies

    b. ethnobotanies

    c. biologies

    d. ethnographies

    e. anthropologies

12. The study of two or more cultures is called a/an _____.

    a. ethnology

    b. case study

    c. ethnography

    d. biography

    e. ethnohistory

13. Anthropologists doing fieldwork typically involve themselves in many different experiences. They try to investigate not just one aspect of culture (such as the political system) but how all aspects relate to each other (for example, how the political system fits with economic institutions, religious beliefs, etc.). This approach is called the _____ perspective.

    a. holistic

    b. ethnological

    c. sociocultural

    d. sociological

    e. culture-bound

14. Ethnographic fieldwork _____.

    a. is usually associated with the study of wealthy elites

    b. is usually associated with the study of North American society

    c. is usually associated with the study of non-Western peoples

    d. can be applied, with useful results, to the study of North American peoples

    e. "is usually associated with the study of non-Western peoples" and "can be applied, with useful results, to the study of North American peoples"

15. In Japan organ transplants are _____.
    a. very common
    b. common among the middle classes only
    c. practiced only among anonymous givers
    d. rarely performed
    e. absolutely never performed

16. Besides being interested in descriptions of particular cultures, the ethnologist is interested in _____.
    a. teaching food foragers how to use time saving gadgets
    b. cross-cultural comparisons
    c. descriptions of nonhuman species
    d. promoting Western ways
    e. providing data to various government agencies to help them suppress certain groups

17. The goal of science is _____.
    a. to discover the universal principles that govern the workings of the visible world
    b. to develop explanations of the world that are testable and correctable
    c. to eliminate the need to use the imagination
    d. "to discover the universal principles that govern the workings of the visible world", "to develop explanations of the world that are testable and correctable" and "to eliminate the need to use the imagination"
    e. "to discover the universal principles that govern the workings of the visible world" and "to develop explanations of the world that are testable and correctable"

18. Short-term changes in response to a particular environmental stimulus are called _____.
    a. biocultural connections
    b. developmental adaptations
    c. physiological adaptations
    d. molecular adaptations
    e. none of the above

19. Which of the following was/were pioneers in visual anthropology?
    a. Clyde Snow, Franz Boas
    b. Clyde Snow, Suzanne Leclerc-Madlala
    c. Franz Boas, Matilda Coxe Stevenson
    d. Matilda Coxe Stevenson, Suzanne Leclerc-Madlala
    e. William Haviland, Franz Boas

20. On which of the following are theories in cultural anthropology usually based?
    a. intensive fieldwork done in a single society
    b. ethnographies from all over the world so that statements made about culture will be universally applicable

c. worldwide questionnaire surveys

d. intuitive thinking about society and culture based on experiences in one's own society

e. the theories about culture formulated by the people one has studied

21. In the process of doing research, ethnographers involve themselves intensively in the lives of those they study, trying to experience culture from their informants' points of view. In this sense, anthropology is _____.

a. scientific

b. humanistic

c. radical

d. conservative

e. systematic

22. In the writing and dissemination of research material the anthropologist has to consider obligations to various entities. Which of the following would *not* be one of the groups the anthropologist would be obligated to?

a. the profession of anthropology

b. the people who funded the study

c. the people studied

d. the anthropologist's parents

e. none of these

23. Linguistic anthropology is concerned with _____.

a. the description of language

b. the history of language

c. how language reflects a people's understanding of the world around them

d. "the description of language" and "the history of language"

e. "the description of language", "the history of language" and "how language reflects a people's understanding of the world around them"

24. Current estimates place the number of HIV/AIDS victims worldwide at _____.

a. 4 million

b. 17 million

c. 65 million

d. 150 million

e. 40 million

25. Which of the following organizations works to examine and modify the practice of anthropology in our changing world?

a. American Anthropological Institute

b. Associated Anthropological Union

c. American Anthropological Association

d. Anthropological Association of America

e. Association of American Anthropologists

26. It was not until the late _____ century that a significant number of Europeans considered the behavior of others different from them to be at all relevant to an understanding of themselves.
    a. nineteenth
    b. twentieth
    c. seventeenth
    d. fourteenth
    e. eighteenth

27. Which of the following is not a driving force behind globalization today?
    a. lower communication costs
    b. higher transportation costs
    c. technological innovations
    d. faster knowledge transfers
    e. increased international financial integration

28. Another name for physical anthropology is _____.
    a. primatology
    b. evolutionary biology
    c. bio-ecology
    d. biological anthropology
    e. forensic anthropology

29. Although humans are all members of a single species, we differ from each other in some obvious and not so obvious ways. Which of the following would be ways that human differ?
    a. skin color
    b. the shape of various physical features
    c. biochemical factors
    d. susceptibility to certain diseases
    e. "skin color," "the shape of various physical features," "biochemical factors," and "susceptibility to certain diseases"

30. According to your text, we may think of culture as the often unconscious standards by which groups of people operate. These standards are _____.
    a. genetically transmitted
    b. biologically inherited
    c. learned
    d. absorbed by osmosis
    e. none of these

31. Which of the following is not a specialty of physical anthropology?
    a. cultural resource management
    b. molecular anthropology

   c. primatology

   d. human evolutionary studies

   e. paleoanthropology

32. The archaeologist is able to find out about human behavior in the past, far beyond the mere _____ years to which historians are limited, by their dependence upon written records.

   a. 20,000

   b. 10,000

   c. 5,000

   d. 7,000

   e. 8,000

33. Anthropological research techniques are applicable for which of the following research subjects?

   a. the study of non-western peoples

   b. the study of health care delivery systems

   c. schools

   d. corporate bureaucracies

   e. "the study of non-western peoples," "the study of health care delivery systems," "schools," and "corporate bureaucracies"

34. _____ is/are another hallmark of anthropology.

   a. Case studies

   b. Surveys

   c. Random sampling

   d. Cross-cultural comparisons

   e. None of these

35. Another name for the ethnographic method is _____.

   a. participant observation

   b. ethnography

   c. ethnology

   d. case studies

   e. none of these

36. One well known forensic anthropologist is _____.

   a. Sheila Brooks

   b. Bernardo Arriaza

   c. Jennifer Thompson

   d. Clyde C. Snow

   e. none of these

37. From skeletal remains, the forensic anthropologist can not establish which of following?
    a. stature
    b. race
    c. sex
    d. marital status
    e. age

38. A pioneering American anthropologist, who did work among the Zuni and founded the Women's Anthropological Society in 1885.
    a. Margaret Mead
    b. Ruth Benedict
    c. Martha Knack
    d. Margaret Lyneis
    e. Matilda Coxe Stevenson

39. _____ worked among immigrant populations in the United States in order to combat racism.
    a. Franz Boas
    b. Bronislaw Malinowski
    c. John Wesley Powell
    d. Leslie White
    e. Fredric Ward Putnam

40. An explanation of natural phenomena supported by a reliable body of data is a[n] _____.
    a. hypothesis
    b. theory
    c. fact
    d. imagination
    e. symbol

41. Which of the following services is **not** one that forensic anthropologists are routinely called upon by the police and other authorities to do?
    a. identify potential archaeological sites
    b. identify the remains of murder victims
    c. identify missing persons
    d. identify people who have died in disasters
    e. identify victims of genocide

42. Among the skeletal remains studied by forensic anthropologist Clyde Snow are the remains of _____.
    a. Julius Caesar
    b. General George A. Custer
    c. Adolf Hitler

    d. Josef Mengele

    e. General George A. Custer and Josef Mengele

43. This woman anthropologist was hired by the Bureau of American Ethnology in 1888, making her one of the first women in the U.S. to receive a full-time position in science.

    a. Margaret Mead

    b. Ruth Benedict

    c. Matilda Coxe Stevenson

    d. Laura Nader

    e. Martha Knack

44. _____ and his students made anthropology courses a common part of college and university curricula.

    a. John Wesley Powell

    b. Fredric Ward Putnam

    c. Bronislaw Malinowski

    d. Claude Levi-Strauss

    e. Franz Boas

45. Which of the following is a hallmark of anthropological research?

    a. library research

    b. writing books

    c. lecturing

    d. fieldwork

    e. administering questionnaires

46. Although the sciences and humanities are often thought of as mutually exclusive approaches they do share some common methods for certain activities. Which of the following activities is not common to both the humanities and sciences?

    a. critical thinking

    b. mental creativity

    c. innovation

    d. data gathering

    e. none of these

47. The authors of your textbook, has identified two countries that have made moves toward allowing same sex unions. Identify the two countries.

    a. Mexico and Sweden

    b. Belgium and the Netherlands

    c. Afghanistan and Pakistan

    d. Italy and Greece

    e. The United States and Canada

48. The terrorist attacks on the World Trade Center and the Pentagon would be of primary interest to which sub-discipline of anthropology?
    a. archaeology
    b. economic anthropology
    c. ethnology
    d. forensic anthropology
    e. medical anthropology

49. As shown in your textbook, forensic anthropologist _____ works at piecing together the remains of victims of state-sponsored terrorism in Argentina.
    a. Franz Boas
    b. Clyde Snow
    c. Matilda Coxe Stevenson
    d. John Wesley Powell
    e. William Haviland

50. _____ theories about the world and reality are based on assumptions and values of one's own culture.
    a. Culturally relative
    b. Physiological
    c. Culture-bound
    d. Applied
    e. Molecular

51. Made possible by means of sophisticated communications, human cultures developed the physical capacity for which of the following?
    a. tool use
    b. mental telepathy
    c. complex language
    d. accumulating wealth
    e. A and C

52. Anthropologists do their work within _____ subfields of the discipline.
    a. one
    b. two
    c. ten
    d. seven
    e. four

53. In anthropology, tentative explanations of observed phenomena concerning humankind are known as _____.
    a. theories
    b. hypotheses

c. opinions

d. patterns

e. facsimiles

54. As experts in the anatomy of human bones and tissues, _____ lend their knowledge about the body to applied areas such as gross anatomy laboratories and to criminal investigations.

    a. ethnographers

    b. linguistic anthropologists

    c. ethnologists

    d. physical anthropologists

    e. archaeologists

55. The study of living and fossil primates falls with the purview of _____.

    a. primatology

    b. osteology

    c. paleopathology

    d. forensic anthropology

    e. archaeology

56. Which of the following areas would not be of interest to the physical anthropologist?

    a. genes and genetic relationships

    b. growth and development

    c. human evolution

    d. political behavior

    e. human adaptation

57. If I were called by the local police department's crime scene investigation unit to identify a murder victim, I would probably be a _____.

    a. medical anthropologist

    b. forensic anthropologist

    c. paleoanthropologist

    d. paleoarchaeologist

    e. forensic entymologist

58. Using anthropological knowledge and methods to solve practical problems falls within the realm of _____.

    a. ethnology

    b. ethnography

    c. medical anthropology

    d. forensic anthropology

    e. applied anthropology

59. Explanations for natural or cultural phenomena, supported by a reliable body of data are known as _____.
    a. notions
    b. inspirations
    c. theories
    d. hypotheses
    e. factoids

60. One may think of ethnology as the study of alternative ways of doing things. Moreover, by making systematic comparisons, ethnologists seek to arrive at scientific conclusions concerning the _____.
    a. healing traditions and practices
    b. relationship between language and culture
    c. function and operation of culture in all times and places
    d. human evolution
    e. enzymes, hormones, and other molecules

61. The Garbage Project was designed in order to study each of the following except:
    a. contemporary social issues
    b. religious and ethnic affiliations
    c. validity of survey techniques
    d. differences in people's perceptions of reality
    e. waste disposal challenges

62. The branch of archaeology tied to government policies for the protection of cultural resources is called:
    a. cultural resource management
    b. forensic anthropology
    c. molecular anthropology
    d. museology
    e. contract archaeology

True/False Practice Questions

1. Culture is preserved and transmitted by language and observation.
   True or False

2. While ethnography is the in-depth study of a single culture, ethnology is the comparative study of culture.
   True or False

3. Ethnographic fieldwork is never done in Western societies.
   True or False

4. Anthropology can best be defined as the cross-cultural study of social behavior.
   True or False

5. Forensic anthropologists are particularly interested in the use of anthropological information for the purpose of debate, oratory and rhetorical criticism.
   True or False

6. A forensic anthropologist can even tell from skeletal remains whether the deceased was right or left handed.
   True or False

7. What a forensic anthropologist cannot tell from skeletal remains are details of an individual's health and nutritional history.
   True or False

8. Besides providing factual accounts of the fate of victims who had disappeared (*desparecidos*) to their surviving kin, Snow's work helped convict several Argentine military officers of kidnapping, torture, and murder.
   True or False

9. All cases of forensic anthropologists involve the abuse of police powers, and evidence provided by them is often ancillary to bringing the guilty party to justice.
   True or False

10. Franz Boas was the first to teach anthropology in the United States.
    True or False

11. Since the subject matter of anthropology is vast, a single anthropologist is personally able to investigate everything that has to do with people.
    True or False

12. Anthropologists know that if formulated correctly their theories will be completely beyond challenge.
    True or False

13. Archaeologists are physical anthropologists.
    True or False

14. Ethnologists study languages throughout time to determine how they have changed.
    True or False

15. Anthropologists think of their findings as something apart from those of other social scientists.
    True or False

16. The subdisciplines of physical and cultural anthropology are closely related, since we cannot understand what people do unless we know what people are.
    True or False

17. Physical anthropologists just study fossil skulls, they would not be interested in studying the recently deceased.
    True or False

18. According to anthropological research, in North American society the ever-increasing amount of household appliance consumer goods has in fact resulted in a steady reduction in household work, with a consequent increase in leisure time.
    True or False

19. In a sense, one may think of ethnology as the study of alternative ways of doing things.
    True or False

20. No-where in the world have anthropologist documented same-sex marriages. In all human societies such unions are not deemed appropriate under any circumstances.
    True or False

21. Cultural and physical anthropologists share common interests in the interplay between human culture and biology.
    True or False

22. Because their differences are distributed independently, humans cannot be classified into races having any biological validity.
    True or False

23. According to your textbook, traditional healers in South Africa are vital to the fight against HIV/AIDS in that area.
    True or False

24. Anthropologists work within at least 10 subfields of the discipline of anthropology.
    True or False

25. Though each of the four subdisciplines of anthropology has its own research strategies, they rely upon each other and are united by a common anthropological perspective on the human condition.
    True or False

26. The main aim of anthropologists is to develop reliable theories about the human species.
    True or False

27. Linguistic anthropology focuses primarily on the cultural aspects of language, and as such has no connection with the discipline of physical anthropology.
    True or False

28. Biologically, humans are apes. That is, they are large bodied, broad shouldered primates with no tails.
    True or False

29. Detailed studies of the hormonal, genetic, and the physiological basis of healthy growth in living humans contributes only to our understanding of the growth patterns of our ancestors, and has nothing to do with the health of children today.
    True or False

30. Humans, because they differ from each other in many ways, can be categorized into several species.
    True or False

31. As long as a theory is widely accepted by the international community of scholars, it is beyond change.
    True or False

32. Generally, globalization has brought significant gains to higher-educated groups in wealthier countries, while doing little to boost developing countries and actually, contributing to the erosion of traditional cultures.
    True or False

33. In this age of globalization, anthropology may not only provide humanity with useful insights concerning diversity, but it may also assist us in avoiding or overcoming significant problems born of that diversity.
True or False

34. Differences in skin color are simply surface adaptations to differing amounts of ultraviolet radiation and have nothing to do with physical or mental capabilities.
True or False

35. Human "races" are nothing more than folk categories, and the sooner everyone recognizes that the categories lack scientific merit, the better off we will all be.
True or False

36. Organ transplantation is the biological movement of an organ from one individual to another.
True or False

Practice Matching

1. _____ Anthropology
2. _____ Physical anthropology
3. _____ Cultural anthropology
4. _____ Forensic anthropology
5. _____ Culture-bound
6. _____ Archaeology

a. Field of applied physical anthropology that specializes in the identification of human skeletal remains for legal purposes.
b. The systematic study of humans as biological organisms.
c. The study of humankind, in all times and places.
d. The branch of anthropology that focuses on human behavior.
e. The study of material remains, usually from the past, to describe and explain human behavior.
f. Theories about the world and reality based on the assumptions and values of one's own culture.

Practice Essays

1. Illustrate the usefulness of ethnographic fieldwork in North American society by discussing research on the infant sleeping patterns.

2. Discuss the characteristics of participant-observation and how this method contributes to ethnographic understanding. How is this method characteristically different from other methods of social science research?

3. Describe how anthropology is, at the same time, a social/behavioral science, a natural science, and one of the humanities.

4. Stephen Jay Gould said, "The greatest impediment to scientific innovation is usually a conceptual lock, not a factual lock." Explain what is meant by this.

5. Your textbook gives different examples to illustrate the relevance of anthropological knowledge in the contemporary world. Identify and describe those examples.

6. How does the work of medical anthropology serve the interests of public health?

7. What are some of the difficulties that arise when applying the scientific approach in anthropology?

8. How can a cultural practice affect human biology? Explain.

9. Who is Clyde Snow? Describe his work.

10. What is "brain death" and how do Japanese and North Americans view this medical state differently?

11. Describe the work of the various types of anthropologists.

12. Humans are the only species capable of studying themselves and the world around them. Explain why humans would want to study themselves.

13. Identify Suzanne Leclerc-Madlala and describe her research.

14. What is the difference between scientific theories and hypotheses? Explain by using examples from your textbook.

15. Discuss the pros and cons of the issue of same sex marriage.

16. Providing examples, explain why the distinction between nation and state is important.

Solutions

Fill-in-the-Blank

1. humankind
2. 150
3. biological
4. physical, cultural, linguistics, archaeology
5. forensic
6. material
7. ethnography
8. food foragers
9. hypothesis
10. participant observation
11. archaeology
12. biological
13. biology
14. molecular anthropology
15. globalization
16. nations

Multiple-Choice Practice Questions

1. B
2. E
3. E
4. B
5. D
6. C
7. E
8. E
9. D
10. A
11. D
12. A
13. A
14. E
15. D
16. B
17. E
18. C
19. C
20. B
21. B
22. D
23. E
24. E
25. C
26. E
27. B
28. D
29. E
30. C
31. A
32. C
33. E
34. D
35. A
36. D
37. D
38. E
39. A
40. B
41. A
42. E
43. C
44. E
45. D
46. D
47. B
48. D
49. B
50. C
51. E
52. E
53. B
54. D
55. A
56. D
57. B
58. E
59. C
60. C
61. B
62. A

True/False Practice Questions

1. T
2. T
3. F
4. F
5. F
6. T
7. F
8. T
9. F
10. F
11. F
12. F
13. F
14. F
15. F
16. T
17. F
18. F
19. T
20. F
21. T
22. T

23.	T	30.	F	**Practice Matching**	
24.	F	31.	F	1.	C
25.	T	32.	T	2.	B
26.	T	33.	T	3.	D
27.	F	34.	T	4.	A
28.	T	35.	T	5.	F
29.	F	36.	F	6.	E

Chapter 2

Characteristics of Culture

Synopsis

Challenge Issues: What is culture? Why do cultures exist? Are some cultures better than others? This chapter presents the fundamental anthropological concept of culture. It is learned, shared, based on symbols, integrated as a well-structured system, and dynamic. Through culture and its many constructions, the human species has secured not only its survival but its expansion as well, using culture as a primary tool for individual and social adaptation. The chapter concludes by considering whether it is possible for anthropologists to evaluate and compare cultures.

Chapter Objectives

   I.   the concept of culture

  II.   characteristics of culture

 III.   culture, society, and the individual

 IV.   evaluation of culture

Key Terms

cultural relativism	infrastructure
culture	pluralistic society
enculturation	social structure
ethnic group	society
ethnicity	subculture
ethnocentrism	superstructure
gender	symbol

Exercises

Review Questions

1. What are five characteristics of culture, according to your text?

2. Distinguish between "culture" and "society." Do they always go together?

3. Distinguish between sex and gender.

4. Give an example of a pluralistic society, and consider what factors seem to allow the larger culture to tolerate subcultural variation.

5. How is culture transmitted?

6. What is meant by the "integration" of various aspects of culture? Give an example.

7. How was anthropology able to contribute to the architectural problems of the Apache Indians?

8. What is the role of enculturation in the transmission of culture?

9. How did Malinowski define the "needs" to be fulfilled by all cultures?

10. What can anthropologists learn about ancient social structure from burials?

11. What is the difference between an ethnic group and a subculture?

12. What changes have recently impacted many pastoralists in sub-Saharan Africa?

13. In what ways must a balance be struck between society and the individuals who comprise it?

14. How can the large-scale sacrifices of the Aztec be explained?

15. Distinguish between ethnocentrism and cultural relativism.

16. According to Walter Goldschmidt, what aspects of society indicate how well the physical and psychological needs of its people are being met?

17. What was E. B. Tylor's original definition of culture in 1871? (This is a classic definition in anthropology, so you should be familiar with it).

18. Approximately how old is human culture?

Fill-in-the-Blank

1. The culture concept was first developed in the _____ century.

2. Your text defines culture as "a society's shared and socially transmitted ideas, _____, and _____, used to make sense of experience and which generate behavior and are reflected in that behavior."

3. When groups function within a society with their own distinctive standards of behavior, we speak of _____ variation.

4. Enculturation refers to the process through which culture is transmitted from one _____ to the next.

5. Cultural elaborations and meanings assigned to the biological differentiation between the sexes is called _____.

6. Another name for a multi-ethnic society is a _____ society.

7. In Kapauku culture, gardens of _____ supply most of the food, but it is through breeding pigs that a man achieves political power.

8. There is a difference between what people say the rules are and actual behavior; that is, the anthropologist must distinguish between the _____ and the real.

9. The most important symbolic aspect of culture is _____.

10. Most organisms adapt by acquiring changes in their _____.

11. Pastoral nomadic people in Africa south of the _____ have survived droughts because of their mobility.

12. The members of all societies consider their own culture to be the best; thus all people can be said to be _____.

13. Anthropology tries to promote cultural _____, or the idea that a culture must be evaluated according to its own standards.

Multiple-Choice Practice Questions

1. The contemporary definition of culture has changed from the meaning given to it during the nineteenth century. Today, _____.
   a. culture is seen as values and beliefs that lie behind behavior rather than as actual behavior.
   b. culture is seen as real rather than as ideal
   c. the term "culture" has been replaced by the term "society."
   d. culture is defined as objects rather than ideas
   e. the term "culture" is not used

2. One way to determine if people share the same culture is to observe whether they _____.
   a. are dependent on each other for survival
   b. are able to interpret and predict each other's actions
   c. live in the same territory
   d. behave in an identical manner
   e. all of the above

3. Which of the following statements about society and culture is **incorrect**?
   a. Culture can exist without a society
   b. A society can exist without culture
   c. Ants and bees have societies but no culture
   d. A culture is shared by the members of a society
   e. Although members of a society may share a culture, their behavior is not uniform

4. Every culture teaches its members that there are differences between people based on sex, age, occupation, class, and ethnic group. People learn to predict the behavior of people playing different roles from their own. This means that _____.
   a. culture is shared even though everyone is not the same
   b. everyone plays the same role
   c. all cultures identify the same roles
   d. all cultures require that their participants play different roles, even though that means that no one can predict the behavior of others
   e. everyone plays the same role throughout his or her life

5. The cultural definitions of what it means to be a male or female today _____.
   a. are determined by biological differences
   b. are independent of biological differences
   c. stem from biological differences that today are relatively insignificant
   d. developed about 60 million years ago
   e. have no relationship to sex

6. When groups function within a society with their own distinctive standards of behavior, we speak of _____.
   a. subcultural variation
   b. social structure

   c. gender differences

   d. cultural materialism

   e. ethnocentrism

7. The Amish may be used as an example of a/an _____.

   a. pluralistic society

   b. subculture

   c. integrated society

   d. world culture

   e. complex society

8. The process by which culture is transmitted from one generation to the next is _____.

   a. enculturation

   b. pluralism

   c. adaptation

   d. cultural relativism

   e. subcultural variation

9. Which of the following statements is **incorrect**?

   a. All culture is learned

   b. All learned behavior is cultural

   c. Culture is humankind's "social heredity."

   d. Culture is not biologically inherited

   e. The process whereby culture is transmitted from one generation to the next is called enculturation

10. The most important symbolic aspect of culture is _____.

   a. art

   b. language

   c. religion

   d. money

   e. politics

11. Among the Kapauku Papuans of New Guinea, the fact that an attempt to eliminate warfare (Which would create a balanced sex ratio) would affect the practice of polygyny, which would affect the economy (since women raise pigs, and the more wives a man has the more pigs he can keep), shows that culture is _____.

   a. materialistic

   b. relative

   c. pluralistic

   d. integrated

   e. enculturated

12. Which of the following is not a characteristic of culture?
    a. shared
    b. learned
    c. based on symbols
    d. fixed
    e. integrated

13. Which of the following is the least restrictive society in terms of rules of sexual conduct?
    a. Kapauku
    b. Canela
    c. Amish
    d. Muslim Brotherhood
    e. Norwegians

14. The process by which organisms adjust beneficially to their environment, or the characteristics by which they overcome hazards and gain access to the resources they need to survive, is called _____.
    a. culture
    b. biology
    c. social structure
    d. integration
    e. adaptation

15. Behavior can be adaptive in the short run but maladaptive in the long run. In the Central Valley in California, vast irrigation projects have created a garden, but salts and chemicals accumulating in the soil will eventually create another desert. This same process occurred in _____.
    a. Mexico
    b. Morocco
    c. ancient Mesopotamia
    d. Great Britain
    e. the Yellow River Valley of China

16. A culture must satisfy basic needs such as _____.
    a. the distribution of necessary goods and services
    b. biological continuity through reproduction and enculturation of functioning adults
    c. maintenance of order within a society and between a society and outsiders
    d. motivation to survive
    e. all of the above

17. _____ refers to the position that because cultures are unique, each one should be evaluated according to its own standards and values.
    a. Ethnocentrism
    b. Cultural relativism

c. Cultural materialism

d. Adaptation

e. Pluralism

18. Goldschmidt suggests that it is possible to decide which cultures are more successful than others by looking at which ones _____.

a. survive

b. last the longest

c. satisfy the physical and cultural needs of the people

d. support the most people

e. are the least emotional

19. A mountain people of western New Guinea studied in 1955 by the North American anthropologist Leo Pospisil.

a. !Kung San

b. Kaluli

c. Basseri

d. Kapauku

e. Azande

20. We now know that any culture that is functioning adequately regards itself as the best, a view reflecting a phenomenon known as _____.

a. cultural relativism

b. egoism

c. nationalisti

d. ethnocentrism

e. individualism

21. The idea that one must suspend judgment on other peoples' practices in order to understand them in their own cultural terms is called _____.

a. structuralism

b. functionalism

c. structural functionalism

d. cultural relativism

e. relative culturalism

22. In regards to the concept of cultural relativism, anthropologist _____ emphasized that ". . . one does not avoid making judgments, but rather postpones them in order to make informed judgments later."

a. David Maybury-Lewis

b. Daniel Day-Lewis

c. Francis L. K. Shu

d. E. E. Evans-Pritchard

e. A. F. C. Wallace

23. As a result of _____ work, in 1981, the Apaches were able to move into houses that had been designed with their participation, for their specific needs.
    a. Walter Goldschmidt's
    b. George Esber's
    c. David Maybury-Lewis's
    d. Bronislaw Kasper Malinowski's
    e. Margaret Mead's

24. The British anthropologist _____ was the originator of what has come to be known as the functionalist school of thought.
    a. Claude Levi-Strauss
    b. George Simmel
    c. Bronislaw Malinowski
    d. Leslie A. White
    e. Ruth Benedict

25. _____ is a gradual process by which organisms adapt to the conditions of the locality in which they live.
    a. adjustment
    b. adaptation
    c. mutation
    d. transformation
    e. vasoconstriction

26. To insure survival of a group of people, a culture must do which of the following?
    a. satisfy the basic needs of those who live by its rules
    b. provide for its own continuity
    c. provide an orderly existence for members of a society
    d. have the capacity to change
    e. all of the above

27. At the ancient Maya city of Tikal, excavations revealed that _____
    a. skeletal type was not related to height variables in the population
    b. height did not vary within the population of inhabitants
    c. diet and nutrition correlated directly with social status and height
    d. upper class individuals never redistributed food to lower class individuals
    e. burials were the same for all members of society

28. In 1871, _____ defined culture as "that complex whole which includes knowledge, belief, art, law, morals, custom and any other capabilities and habits acquired by man as a member of society.
    a. A. L. Kroeber
    b. Clyde Kluckhohn

    c. Edward Burnett Tylor

    d. Karl Marx

    e. Margaret Mead

29. Which of the following is **not** a characteristic of society?

    a. A group of people who share a common homeland

    b. A group of people who are dependent on each other for survival

    c. A group of people who share a culture

    d. A group of people who share a common identity

    e. All of the above are characteristic of a society

30. To survive, a culture must _____.

    a. satisfy the basic needs of those who live by its rules

    b. provide for its own continuity

    c. furnish an orderly existence for the members of its society

    d. strike a balance between the self-interests of individuals and the needs of society as a whole

    e. all of the above

31. Gender differences are as old as human culture, or about _____ years.

    a. 5 million

    b. 2.5 million

    c. 100,000

    d. 250,000

    e. 1 million

32. The thesis that one must suspend judgment on other peoples' practices to understand them in their own cultural terms.

    a. Ethnocentrism

    b. Separatism

    c. Social relativism

    d. Socialism

    e. Cultural relativism

33. The job of anthropologists is to abstract a set of rules from what they observe to explain the social behavior of a people. To arrive at a realistic description of a culture free from personal and cultural biases, anthropologists must _____.

    a. make judgments on other peoples' practices to understand them

    b. examine a people's notion of the way their society ought to function

    c. determine how a people think they behave

    d. compare how people think they ought to behave with how they actually behave

    e. "examine a people's notion of the way their society ought to function", "determine how a people think they behave", "compare how people think they ought to behave with how they actually behave"

34. Although citizens of the United States are fond of boasting that theirs is the finest health care system in the world, they are merely reflecting _____ of their own culture.
    a. nationalism
    b. cultural relativism
    c. ethnocentrism
    d. relativism
    e. euphemism

35. Through culture, the human species has secured not just its survival but its expansion. Which of the following would be examples of human expansion?
    a. settlements in the Arctic region
    b. flights to the moon
    c. settlements in the Sahara Desert
    d. the exploration of space
    e. "settlements in the Arctic region", "flights to the moon", "settlements in the Sahara Desert" and "the exploration of space"

36. Because subsistence practices involve tapping into available resources to satisfy a society's basic needs, this aspect of culture is known as _____.
    a. infrastructure
    b. subculture
    c. social structure
    d. superstructure
    e. acculturation

37. _____ was a pioneer in anthropological fieldwork techniques.
    a. George Esber
    b. George Peter Murdock
    c. Leslie White
    d. A. R. Radcliffe-Brown
    e. Bronislaw Malinowski

38. Among the Kapauku, descent reckoning through men, coupled with near-constant warfare, tends to promote _____.
    a. egalitarianism
    b. female dominance
    c. male dominance
    d. dictatorship
    e. cultural deviance

True/False Practice Questions

1. To say that culture is shared means that all members of a society behave in the same way.
   True or False

2. A pluralistic society always has subcultural variation, but not every society with subcultural variation is pluralistic.
   True or False

3. A larger culture is more likely to tolerate a subculture if their values and physical appearances are similar.
   True or False

4. Cattle herding is the mainstay around which all of Kapauku Papuan society revolves.
   True or False

5. A modern definition of culture emphasizes the values, beliefs, and rules that lie behind behavior rather than the actual observable behavior itself.
   True or False

6. Cultures are dynamic systems.
   True or False

7. The Amish are an ethnic group in the United States.
   True or False

8. There are some societies that have no regulation of sex whatsoever.
   True or False

9. There can be no culture without a society.
   True or False

10. Ants and bees instinctively cooperate in a manner that clearly indicates a degree of social organization, therefore they have culture.
    True or False

11. Though one's sex is culturally determined, one's sexual identity or gender is biologically constructed.
    True or False

12. The degree of tolerance accorded the Amish is due in part to the fact that they are "white" Europeans.
    True or False

13. So-called racial characteristics represent biological adaptations to climate and have nothing to do with differences in intelligence or cultural superiority.
    True or False

14. Learned behavior is exhibited to one degree or another by most, if not all, mammals.
    True or False

15. If a society is to survive it must succeed in balancing the self-interest of its members against the demands of the society as a whole.
    True or False

16. Numerous studies by a variety of social scientists have clearly shown that the death penalty does deter violent crime in the United States.
    True or False

17. Cross cultural studies show that homicide rates mostly decline after the death penalty is abolished.
    True or False

18. Deviance is the same in every culture.
    True or False

19. People maintain cultures to deal with problems or matters that concern them.
    True or False

20. A culture must have the capacity to change so it can adapt to altered perceptions of existing circumstances.
    True or False

21. Cultures are biologically inherited, rather than learned.
    True or False

22. Humans do everything because it is adaptive to a particular environment.
    True or False

23. What is adaptive in one context may be seriously maladaptive in another.
    True or False

24. The tricks that pigeons learn are the product of enculturation.
    True or False

25. For a culture to function properly, its various parts must be consistent with each other because consistency means harmony.
    True or False

26. Adult human stature is not affected by culture.
    True or False

27. Anthropologists seldom look at the archaeological or historical record to test hypotheses about culture change.
    True or False

Practice Matching

Match the culture with its description.

1. _____ Amish

2. _____ Trobrianders

3. _____ Kapauku Papuans

4. _____ Aztec

5. _____ Apache

a. A Native American people with distinct architectural needs.

b. A Pacific Island people studied by Malinowski.

c. A pacifist agrarian subculture of the U.S.

d. A New Guinea people who breed pigs.

e. A civilization in Mexico that engaged in large-scale sacrifices.

Short Answer

1. What must be done for a culture to function properly?

2. What is meant by the statement "culture is dynamic?"

3. What happens when a culture is too rigid?

4. Name the five characteristics of culture.

5. Although people maintain cultures to deal with problems, it is clear that some cultural practices prove to be maladaptive and actually create new problems. Provide examples of cultural practices that have proved maladaptive, creating new problems.

6. What is the barrel model of culture?

7. Are animals other than humans capable of culture?

8. Explain why people maintain cultures.

9. What are the three fundamental levels of needs that Malinowski proposed?

Practice Essays

1. Using the Amish as an example of subcultural variation, discuss some of the factors that seem to determine whether or not subcultural variation is tolerated by the larger culture. Compare the Amish to another group that is less well-tolerated.

2. Distinguish between the concepts of culture and society.

3. Discuss the distinction between sex and gender and explain why this distinction is important.

4. Discuss the interrelatedness of the various parts of Kapauku culture. Use examples.

5. How does culture balance the needs of the individual with the needs of society?

6. Provide examples to support the statement, "What is adaptive in one context may be seriously maladaptive in another."

7. Using the example of the Kapauku Papuans, explain the idea that culture is integrated.

8. Anthropologist James Peacock wrote a book called *The Anthropological Lens* in which he compared culture to a lens or glass through which people experience the world. The anthropologist, then, is like an oculist who hopes to find the "formula" of each kind of lens, acquiring a kind of stereoscopy, or depth perception, by being able to perceive things through multiple lenses. How is culture like a lens? What are the limitations of this metaphor for understanding culture and anthropology?

9. What is cultural relativism and how does it impact anthropology as a discipline?

Solutions

Fill-in-the-Blank

1. 19th
2. values, perceptions
3. subcultural
4. generation
5. gender
6. pluralistic
7. sweet potatoes
8. ideal
9. language
10. bodies
11. Sahara
12. ethnocentric
13. relativity

Multiple-Choice Practice Questions

1. A
2. B
3. A
4. A
5. C
6. A
7. B
8. A
9. B
10. B
11. D
12. D
13. B
14. E
15. C
16. E
17. B
18. C
19. D
20. D
21. D
22. A
23. B
24. C
25. B
26. E
27. C
28. C
29. E
30. E
31. B
32. E
33. E
34. C
35. E
36. A
37. E
38. C

True/False Practice Questions

1. F
2. T
3. T
4. F
5. T
6. T
7. F
8. F
9. T
10. F
11. F
12. T
13. T
14. T
15. T
16. F
17. T
18. F
19. T
20. T
21. F
22. F
23. T
24. F
25. T
26. F
27. F

Practice Matching

1. C
2. B
3. D
4. E
5. A

Chapter 3

Ethnographic Research: Its History, Methods, and Theories

Synopsis

Challenge Issues: How and why did ethnographic research evolve? What are ethnographic research methods? How is research related to theory? This chapter examines the beginnings of ethnographic fieldwork and early contributions to the field, highlighting the various stages of ethnographic research. It concludes with a discussion of the importance of theory and ethical obligations of the researcher.

Chapter Objectives

    I.   history of ethnographic research and its uses

   II.   doing ethnography: Cultural Anthropology research methods

  III.   anthropology and its fields

  IV.   ethnology: from description to interpretation and theory

   V.   moral dilemmas and ethical responsibilities in anthropological research

Key Terms

advocacy anthropology

digital ethnography

doctrine

eliciting device

ethnographic fieldwork

ethnohistory

formal interview

Human Relations Area Files (HRAF)

idealist perspective

informal interview

informed consent

key consultant

materialist perspective

multi-sited ethnography

qualitative data

quantitative data

theory

urgent anthropology

Exercises

The Anthropology Resource Center (ARC)

The Anthropology Resource Center is a dynamic, subfield-specific website that provides a wealth of materials for both students and instructors to reinforce key concepts in anthropology. All of the resources and activities encourage students to apply anthropology beyond the textbook and classroom. ARC can be reached through the weblink http://thomsonedu.com/. After selecting the discipline of "Anthropology" under "Humanities and Social Sciences," go directly to ARC for a wide range of resources that bring anthropology to life through pictures, interviews, news items, interactive displays, maps, and more. (This site is passcode-protected for both instructors and students.)

Review Questions

1. What are the main components of cultural anthropology?

2. What is urgent anthropology?

3. Distinguish between ethnology and ethnography.

4. Describe the effects of acculturation.

5. How did anthropology get started as a discipline?

6. Who are the Ayoreo Indians and how has acculturation affected them?

7. What is applied anthropology?

8. Discuss the historical significance of "national character" studies and the study of "cultures-at-a-distance."

9. Who are Ruth Benedict and Margaret Mead?

10. What are the various kinds of research that early anthropologists carried out in contemporary state societies?

11. What is significant about the category of "peasant studies"?

12. Describe the importance of advocacy anthropology.

13. What is multi-sited ethnography? Provide an example.

14. Discuss how globalization has affected the methods of ethnographic research.

15. What are the various steps involved in doing ethnography?

16. What is a key consultant?

17. Distinguish between formal and informal interviews.

18. What is the significance of mapping?

19. Identify Gregory Bates and Margaret Mead. What were there contributions to the discipline?

20. What is subjectivity? How does it affect ethnographic fieldwork?

21. Describe the differences between the field approach of Bronislaw Malinowski and that of Annette Weiner.

22. What is ethnographic reflexivity?

23. What is digital ethnography?

24. Describe and explain the importance of ethnohistory.

25. Distinguish between doctrine and theory.

26. What are the Human Relations Area Files and what do they contribute to Anthropology?

27. What is an idealist perspective? What is a materialist perspective?

28. Why did Yahweh prohibit the consumption of pork? What are Marvin Harris's arguments about this religious phenomenon?

29. Describe the moral dilemmas faced by ethnographic researchers.

30. List the ethical obligations of an ethnographic researcher.

Fill-in-the-Blank

1. _____ is a detailed description of a particular culture primarily based on fieldwork.

2. _____ is the study and analysis of different cultures from a comparative or historical point of view.

3. Salvage anthropology is known also as _____.

4. Asymmetrical culture contact, or _____, is often disruptive to indigenous societies.

5. A _____ is an explanation or interpretation supported by a reliable body of data.

6. An assertion of opinion or belief formally handed down by an authority as true and indisputable is a _____.

7. Digital ethnography is sometimes called _____.

8. Anthropologists who highlight environmental or economic factors as primary in shaping cultures often share a perspective that is considered _____.

9. _____ is a formal recorded agreement between the anthropologist and the research participants.

10. When an anthropologist utilizes a range of methods in various locations of time and space it is known as _____.

11. _____ is the ethnographic study of online "imagined communities."

12. The use of anthropological knowledge and methods to solve practical problems in communities confronting new challenges is _____.

Multiple-Choice Practice Questions

1. Cultural Anthropology includes the scholarly components of _____ and _____.
   a. ethnology, ethnohistory
   b. ethnography, ethnology
   c. ethnohistory, archaeology
   d. linguistics, ethnography
   e. ethno-archaeology, forensic anthropology

2. The first-hand study of culture is called _____.
   a. firsthand methods
   b. anthropology in action
   c. informal interviews
   d. primary research
   e. fieldwork

3. Cultural anthropology emerged as a formal discipline _____.
   a. during the 21st century
   b. during the 18th century
   c. during the wars of independence
   d. during the years of the Industrial Revolution
   e. during the years of colonialism

4. In what decade did anthropologists begin acculturation studies?
   a. 1920s
   b. 1930s
   c. 1940s
   d. 1960s
   e. 1990s

5. Who was the first anthropologist to formally study acculturation?
   a. Emily Thompson
   b. Ruth Benedict
   c. Edward Tylor
   d. Margaret Mead
   e. Bronislaw Malinowski

6. Why was the study of "cultures-at-a-distance" important to anthropology?
   a. it helped control the spread of disease
   b. it helped us prevent direct contact between people from different countries
   c. it helped us understand countries with whom we were at war
   d. it helped us change other governments into more democratic structures
   e. all of the above

7. What surprising conclusions did Alfred Métraux find in his studies of race relations in Brazil?
   a. Brazil is a very modern country that does not make any distinctions in terms of race or class
   b. Brazil is the only country in the world that does not have discriminatory social and political practices
   c. in Brazil dark-skinned individuals always rise to the highest levels of political office
   d. light-skinned individuals in Brazil face systemic social and economic discrimination
   e. dark-skinned individuals in Brazil face systemic social and economic discrimination

8. Which of the following would be classified as a peasant?
   a. a fisherman
   b. a forager
   c. a modern industrialist
   d. a large-scale farmer
   e. a small-scale farmer

9. What do we call research that is community-based and politically involved?
   a. political anthropology
   b. culture-at-a-distance
   c. action anthropology
   d. advocacy anthropology
   e. urgent anthropology

10. By the _____ European colonial powers had lost most of their overseas territories.
   a. 1960s
   b. 1970s
   c. 1940s
   d. 1920s
   e. 1990s

11. Another name for the Meskwaki Indians is the _____.
   a. Hopi Indians
   b. Assiniboin Indians
   c. Creek Indians
   d. Fox Indians
   e. Coyote Indians

12. What is a diasporic population?
   a. a population living and working far from their original homelands
   b. a population working in more than one country
   c. a group of people employed by multi-national corporations
   d. a group of people living under refuge conditions
   e. none of the above

13. Rodolfo Stavenhagen can be classified as a(n) _____.
   a. advocacy anthropologist
   b. ethnoarchaeologist
   c. urgent anthropologist
   d. multi-sited ethnographer
   e. diasporic ethnographer

14. A worldwide interconnected landscape with multiple and intertwining peoples and cultures on the move is called a(n) _____.
    a. anthroscape
    b. identiscape
    c. cyberscape
    d. ethnoscape
    e. globalscape

15. Andrea Louie's study of transnational Chinese identity formation should be classified as a(n) _____.
    a. advocacy ethnography
    b. diasporic ethnography
    c. cyberethnography
    d. multi-sited ethnography
    e. situational ethnography

16. The hallmark of the anthropologist's toolkit is _____.
    a. formal interviews
    b. participant observation
    c. random sampling
    d. surveys and questionnaires
    e. photography

17. Ethnographic fieldwork can best be described as _____.
    a. intensive library research and on-location research
    b. off-site research in multiple areas
    c. intensive on-location research over several periods of time
    d. extended library research
    e. extended on-location research

18. The first step in ethnographic fieldwork is _____.
    a. gathering data from informants
    b. doing preparatory research
    c. choosing a research question
    d. talking to the primary subjects at the research site
    e. doing multi-sited ethnography

19. Approximately how many languages are spoken today throughout the world?
    a. 4,000
    b. 5,000
    c. 6,000
    d. 7,000
    e. 8,000

20. Napoleon Chagnon studied _____ in order to prepare for his work on violence among the Yanomamo.
    a. ecological research on violence
    b. applied natural selection theory
    c. linguistic research on categories of thought and action
    d. structural theories on perception
    e. none of the above

21. The primary research method in ethnographic fieldwork is _____.
    a. informal interviews
    b. participant observation
    c. mapping
    d. archival research
    e. observation

22. Which of the following is **not** a quantitative method?
    a. quantities of crops produced
    b. census data
    c. demographic trends
    d. a personal life history
    e. mortality rates

23. Nonstatistical information is classified as _____.
    a. secondary data
    b. archival research
    c. statistical data
    d. quantitative data
    e. qualitative data

24. Structured question-and-answer sessions are called _____.
    a. secondary data
    b. tertiary interviews
    c. primary interviews
    d. informal interviews
    e. formal interviews

25. Sharing details about one's own family in order to prompt other people to share information is the use of _____.
    a. listening devices
    b. soliciting devices
    c. eliciting devices
    d. extractive interviewing
    e. none of the above

26. "Can you tell me about your childhood?" This is an example of a(n) _____.
    a. informal question
    b. formal question
    c. elicited question
    d. closed question
    e. open-ended question

27. With whom did Margaret Mead do her innovative research using ethnographic film?
    a. Reo Fortune
    b. Gregory Bateson
    c. Howard Bills
    d. Franz Boas
    e. Ruth Benedict

28. Margaret Mead urged anthropologists to _____.
    a. to do more fieldwork in the United States
    b. use GPS units in order to make more precise maps
    c. interview more people in the field
    d. use cameras more effectively in the field
    e. to work as a team with other scholars in order to better analyze the field situation

29. When was the first portable synchronous-sound camera invented?
    a. 1975
    b. 1965
    c. 1950
    d. 1945
    e. 1960

30. Margaret Mead and Gregory Bateson worked collaboratively in Bali from _____.
    a. 1933–1950
    b. 1934–1940
    c. 1936–1938
    d. 1940–1945
    e. 1943–1947

31. Successful fieldwork ultimately depends upon _____.
    a. mutual goodwill
    b. having the right theories
    c. having state of the art technology
    d. getting to know the right people
    e. none of the above

32. William Crocker worked with the _____ for more than 60 months.
    a. Navajo
    b. Fox
    c. Canela
    d. Yanomamo
    e. Agta

33. A researcher's access to a community can be affected by _____.
    a. skin color
    b. ethnicity
    c. age
    d. gender
    e. all of the above

34. _____ is a state in which perceptions vary
    a. Validity
    b. Personality
    c. Objectivity
    d. Subjectivity
    e. None of these

35. In what country do we find the Trobriand Islands?
    a. Papua New Guinea
    b. Indonesia
    c. Burma
    d. Philippines
    e. Japan

36. Who was the anthropologist who did a re-study of the Trobriand Islands?
    a. Sheila Brooks
    b. Bernardo Arriaza
    c. Jennifer Thompson
    d. Annette Weiner
    e. none of these

37. What was the focus of the re-study of the Trobriand Islands?
    a. the chief status and political organization
    b. men's religious activities
    c. economic production
    d. women's productive work
    e. child-rearing

38. In order to minimize the impact of subjectivity, anthropologists must study _____.
    a. the way the people think they should behave
    b. the way the people actually behave
    c. the way the people actually think they behave
    d. what they observe the people doing
    e. all of the above

39. What was the primary type of wealth that women distributed in Trobriand society?
    a. banana leave bundles
    b. yams
    c. shell necklaces
    d. corn
    e. all of the above

40. The use of digital technologies (audio and visual) is a primary part of _____.
    a. cyberethnography
    b. hypermedia ethnography
    c. urgent anthropology
    d. hypergamous ethnography
    e. none of the above

41. Why is reflexivity extremely significant to ethnographic research?
    a. it helps minimize personal and cultural biases
    b. it makes the anthropologists feel better
    c. it provides important data about feelings and emotions
    d. it allows people to see you as human
    e. all of the above

42. Historical ethnography is also called _____.
    a. classical studies
    b. advocacy ethnography
    c. theory
    d. digital ethnography
    e. ethnohistory

43. Digital ethnography is also called _____.
    a. cyberethnography
    b. hypomedia ethnography
    c. hypermedia ethnography
    d. computer ethnography
    e. none of the above

44. _____ is the branch of cultural anthropology that makes cross-cultural comparisons.

    a. ethnocentrism

    b. ethnicity

    c. ethnohistory

    d. ethnography

    e. ethnology

45. _____ is an assertion of opinion or belief.

    a. A hypothesis

    b. Theory

    c. Fact

    d. Doctrine

    e. all of the above

46. What do we call the database of cross-cultural ethnographic and archaeological data?

    a. Human Cultures Area Files

    b. Culture Area Data Files

    c. Anthropology Database

    d. Human Relations Area Files

    e. Human Relatives Area Files

47. What is the primary advantage of the HRAF?

    a. it allows people to do ethnographic research without going to the field

    b. it provides cross-cultural data for comparison

    c. it helps us improve our methodology

    d. it allows for studies of cultures-at-a-distance

    e. all of the above

48. Marxism, neo-evolutionism, and cultural ecology are examples of a _____ perspective.

    a. ecological

    b. ideal

    c. idealist

    d. materialist

    e. substantivist

49. Which anthropologist studied the incidence of pork prohibitions in Judaism?

    a. Franz Boas

    b. Marvin Harris

    c. Margaret Mead

    d. John Wesley Powell

    e. William Haviland

50. _____ may be written or oral but should be obtained before continuing with fieldwork.

    a. Informal interviews

    b. Informal consensus

    c. Informed consent

    d. Informed consensus

    e. Informal consent

True/False Practice Questions

1. Many indigenous groups in the United States and Canada have been described as internal colonies.
    True or False

2. Anthropologists have never utilized ethnocentric categories.
    True or False

3. Bronislaw Malinowski was a form opponent of applied anthropology.
    True or False

4. "Culture-at-a-distance" studies were a dismal failure in anthropology.
    True or False

5. Hortense Powdermaker studied media exposure ion Broadway.
    True or False

6. Peasants are the largest social category in the world.
    True or False

7. All anthropologists practice advocacy anthropology in their study site.
    True or False

8. Multi-sited ethnographic research is a growing trend in anthropology.
    True or False

9. In our fast-changing and globalized world, anthropological research methods no longer have anything in common with the way they were initially developed.
    True or False

10. Holistic research through participant observation is no longer the primary goal of ethnographies.
    True or False

11. Anthropologists rarely do preparatory research before entering the field in order to prevent bases in their data collection.
    True or False

12. Participant observation is the primary research tool for all anthropologists, regardless of their historical time period.
    True or False

13. Formal interviews are the most significant form of researcher-consultant interaction in anthropology.
    True or False

14. When a key consultant tells a story about her childhood, it is an example of an eliciting device.
    True or False

15. Good researchers do not face fieldwork differences because of their gender.
    True or False

16. Subjectivity plays a significant role in ethnographic fieldwork.
    True or False

17. Anthropologists who are well trained do not have to worry about subjectivity concerns.
    True or False

18. Margaret Mead worked in the Trobriand Islands and did a re-study in the 1970s.
    True or False

19. Women amass large quantities of banana leaves for trade and accumulation of status in the Trobriand Islands.
    True or False

20. Ethnohistory is the study of contemporary ethnic groups.
    True or False

21. Digital ethnography is an important part of anthropology.
    True or False

22. Validity is an important goal in anthropological research.
    True or False

Practice Matching

1. _____ ethnography
2. _____ ethnology
3. _____ urgent anthropology
4. _____ ethnohistory
5. _____ ethnographic fieldwork
6. _____ advocacy anthropology

a. a study of cultures of the recent past through oral histories and analysis of the written record

b. the study and analysis of different cultures from a comparative point of view

c. a detailed description of a particular culture based on fieldwork

d. the branch of anthropology that documents endangered cultures

e. extended on-location research

f. research that is community-based and politically involved

Practice Short Answers

1. Describe the two primary scholarly components of cultural anthropology?

2. What is fieldwork?

3. Identify urgent anthropology and provide an example of it.

4. What is acculturation?

5. What contributions did Margaret Mead and Ruth Benedict make to the study of anthropology?

6. What are peasant studies and why are they important to anthropology?

7. Who is Hortense Powdermaker?

8. Describe advocacy anthropology and provide examples of some of the early examples in anthropology.

9. What is multi-sited ethnography? Provide an example.

10. Describe a globalscape.

11. What method of research is the most critical to the formation of an ethnography?

12. Compare and contrast formal and informal interviews.

13. What is the role of subjectivity in ethnographic research?

14. Compare and contrast Bronislaw Malinowski's and Annette Weiner's field studies.

15. What is ethnohistory?

Practice Essays

1. Describe the early history of ethnographic research.

2. What challenges and opportunities are created through the practice of urgent anthropology?

3. Compare and contrast urgent anthropology and applied anthropology.

4. What did anthropologist Bronislaw Malinowski mean when he said, "The anthropologist who is unable to … register the tragic errors committed at times with the best intentions … remains an antiquarian covered with academic dust and in fool's paradise."

5. Describe and discuss some of the early anthropological studies of contemporary state societies. What did they focus on and why?

6. Advocacy anthropology presents both challenges and opportunities to the researcher and subject population. Discuss the pros and cons of advocacy anthropology.

7. What kinds of research techniques would be most useful in a cyberethnography?

8. Why is participation observation central to the practice of ethnography?

9. What are the different kinds of data that anthropologists handle?

10. As fully as possible, describe the role of the key informant in the ethnographic research process.

11. Describe several reasons that might account for differences between the fieldwork experiences of two anthropologists. Use data from the Malinowski-Weiner re-study to support and illustrate your arguments.

12. How do anthropologists attempt to control subjectivity while in the field?

13. What is the difference between theories and doctrine? Explain by using examples from your textbook.

14. Discuss the ethical obligations that anthropologists have while doing ethnographic fieldwork.

Solutions

Fill-in-the-Blank

1. Ethnography
2. Ethnology
3. urgent anthropology
4. acculturation
5. theory
6. doctrine
7. hypermedia ethnography
8. materialist
9. Informed consent
10. multi-sited ethnography
11. cyberethnography
12. applied anthropology

Multiple-Choice Practice Questions

1. B
2. E
3. E
4. B
5. D
6. C
7. E
8. E
9. D
10. A
11. D
12. A
13. A
14. E
15. D
16. B
17. E
18. C
19. C
20. B
21. B
22. D
23. E
24. E
25. C
26. E
27. B
28. D
29. E
30. C
31. A
32. C
33. E
34. D
35. A
36. D
37. D
38. E
39. A
40. B
41. A
42. E
43. C
44. E
45. D
46. D
47. B
48. D
49. B
50. C

True/False Practice Questions

1. T
2. T
3. F
4. F
5. F
6. T
7. F
8. T
9. F
10. F
11. F
12. T
13. F
14. F
15. F
16. T
17. F
18. F
19. T
20. F
21. T
22. T
23. T
24. F
25. T
26. T
27. F
28. T
29. F
30. F

Practice Matching

1. C
2. B
3. D
4. A
5. E
6. F

Chapter 4

Becoming Human: The Origin and Diversity of Our Species

Synopsis

Challenge Issues: To what group if animals do humans belong? When and how did humans evolve? Is the biological concept of race useful for studying physical variation in humans? Chapter 4 introduces the student to the anthropological study of the human evolutionary past through an examination of our closest primate relatives, the chimpanzees and bonobos, as well as the biological, cultural, and ecological changes that occurred through the evolution from *Australopithecus* to modern *Homo sapiens*. The chapter concludes with a discussion of race and the sociocultural means of interpreting human diversity.

Chapter Objectives

    I.   evolution through adaptation

   II.   humans and other primates

 III.   human ancestors

 IV.   human biological variation and the problem of race

Key Terms

adaptation
Australopithecus
bipedalism
evolution
genes
hominoid
Homo erectus
Homo habilis
Lower Paleolithic
Mousterian
multiregional hypothesis

natural selection
Neandertals
Oldowan
paleoanthropologist
primate
primatologist
race
recent African origins hypothesis
species
Upper Paleolithic

Exercises

The Anthropology Resource Center (ARC)

The Anthropology Resource Center is a dynamic, subfield-specific website that provides a wealth of materials for both students and instructors to reinforce key concepts in anthropology. All of the resources and activities encourage students to apply anthropology beyond the textbook and classroom. ARC can be reached through the weblink http://thomsonedu.com/. After selecting the discipline of "Anthropology" under "Humanities and Social Sciences," go directly to ARC for a wide range of resources that bring anthropology to life through pictures, interviews, news items, interactive displays, maps, and more. (This site is passcode-protected for both instructors and students.)

Review Questions

1. Distinguish between the terms evolution, natural selection, and adaptation.

2. What is the importance of cultural adaptation?

3. When did human culture first emerge?

4. Describe some of the early classification schemes used for humans.

5. When did the first mammals appear and what were their characteristics?

6. Describe the evolutionary changes that occurred in primate dentition, sight, and touch and also in the primate brain and skeleton.

7. What was the adaptive advantage in binocular stereoscopic color vision among primates?

8. Describe the social structure of chimpanzee and bonobo communities? How are they alike and how are they different?

9. What is genito-genital rubbing?

10. What experiment did Frans de Waal carry out in order to test for the existence of cultural traditions among different primate groups?

11. What is the role of hunting within chimpanzee communities?

12. Describe sexual activity among chimpanzees and bonobos.

13. How does childhood development differ among bonobo and chimpanzee communities?

14. Identify Jane Goodall and Kinji Imanishi. What are their primary contributions to primatology and our understanding of humans?

15. What are the hallmarks of being human?

16. Discuss the significance of bipedalism. What changes resulted from this change in locomotion?

17. What was the role of meat consumption in human evolution?

18. What is the Oldowan Tool Tradition?

19. What role did tool-making play in human evolution?

20. What migratory patterns were associated with the Genus *Homo*?

21. What evolutionary advantages were conferred on *H. erectus* through the control of fire?

22. Discuss the Neandertal controversy. What are the primary arguments involved in this debate?

23. What is the Mousterian tool tradition? With what group of hominoids is it associated?

24. Describe and discuss the debate surrounding the emergence of modern *Homo sapiens*.

25. Define race and explain the impact that human classification has had on our societies.

Fill-in-the-Blank

1. _____ specialize in the behavior and biology of living primates and their evolutionary history.

2. A _____ is an anthropologist that specializes in the study of human evolutionary history.

3. A complex of ideas, activities, and technologies that enable people to survive and even thrive in their environment is _____.

4. Humans are classified as a _____ because they are members of a subgroup of mammals that also includes lemurs, tarsiers, monkeys, and apes.

5. A group of individuals able to interbreed and produce viable offspring is called a _____.

6. The ability to see the world in three dimensions is called _____.

7. Genito-genital rubbing is typical of _____.

8. Upright walking on two feet is called _____.

9. The first part of the Stone Age was called the _____.

10. Shortly after 2 million years ago the species _____ appeared.

11. The tool industry found among the Neandertals was called _____.

12. The Eve or Out of Africa hypothesis is also called _____.

Multiple-Choice Practice Questions

1. Which of the following studies living primates?
   a. paleontologists
   b. paleoanthropologists
   c. primatologists
   d. ethnologists
   e. apologist

2. Which of the following operates on the level of a population through genetic change?
   a. adjustment
   b. natural variation
   c. adaptation
   d. evolution
   e. natural selection

3. When do paleoanthropologists believe that human culture first emerged?
   a. 1.5 million years ago
   b. 2.0 million years ago
   c. 2.5 million years ago
   d. 3.0 million years ago
   e. 3.5 million years ago

4. What is the basic physical unit of heredity?
   a. genus
   b. species
   c. allele
   d. chromosome
   e. gene

5. When did the earliest primates begin to appear?
   a. 4 million years ago
   b. 23 million years ago
   c. 65 million years ago
   d. 200 million years ago
   e. 435 million years ago

6. What is binocular stereoscopic vision?
   a. the ability to see the world in three dimensions
   b. the ability to see the world in four dimensions
   c. the ability to perceive depth
   d. the ability to hunt animals with visual skill
   e. the ability to see in all types of environments

7. What is the function of the vertebrate skeleton?
   a. provide overall shape to the organism
   b. support soft tissue
   c. protect vital internal organs
   d. all of the above
   e. none of the above

8. Which of the following has the least opposability in hands and feet?
   a. bonobos
   b. baboons
   c. humans
   d. chimpanzees
   e. orangutans

9. Among bonobos _____.
   a. females have significantly lower social rank than males
   b. social rank us determined by birth order of siblings, the eldest frequently becoming the alpha male
   c. leadership skills are developed among young males as a result of their relationships with their father
   d. male rank determines the social order of the group more than female rank
   e. female rank determines the social order of the group more than male rank

10. Among bonobos, genito-genital rubbing is a form of _____.
    a. territorial marking
    b. sexual initiation used by females
    c. sexual initiation used by males
    d. reconciliation
    e. aggression

11. Chimpanzees are the only animals to use _____ in their process of conflict resolution.
    a. genito-genital rubbing
    b. mediation
    c. food
    d. aggression
    e. male dominance

12. What surprising information emerged in primate studies in the 1980s?
    a. that chimpanzees have language
    b. that bonobos are extremely territorial
    c. that chimpanzees are meat-eaters
    d. that chimpanzees form into social colonies
    e. all of the above

13. Which of the following studied the reconciliation efforts among bonobos?
    a. Kinji Imanishi
    b. Jane Goodall
    c. Richard Leakey
    d. Frans de Waal
    e. Louis Leakey

14. Who was the first Western female to study primates?
    a. Birute Galdikas
    b. Jane Goodall
    c. Kinji Imanishi
    d. Dian Fossey
    e. Margaret Mead

15. Which of the following primate females engage in perpetual sexual activity?
    a. rhesus macaques
    b. chimpanzees
    c. bonobos
    d. gorillas
    e. gibbons

16. Who was the first primatologist?
    a. Jane Goodall
    b. Louis Leakey
    c. Kinji Imanishi
    d. Dian Fossey
    e. Charles Darwin

17. Between 5 and 15 million years ago hominoids lived in all of the following areas **except**
    _____.
    a. Africa
    b. North America
    c. Central Asia
    d. Europe
    e. Southeast Asia

18. Between 4 and 5 million years ago, the environment of eastern and southern Africa was primarily composed of _____.
    a. high mountains
    b. broad, flat savannahs
    c. open country and woodlands
    d. deep river valleys
    e. thick rainforest

19. The earliest australopithecine fossils date back to _____.
    a. 4.2 million years
    b. 3.6 million years
    c. 6.7 million years
    d. 1.8 million years
    e. 7.9 million years

20. Bipedalism, as opposed to quadrupedalism, is associated with all of the following changes **except** _____.
    a. increased ability to stand and see predators better
    b. increased ability to carry food
    c. increased ability to use tools as weapons
    d. decreased exposure to direct sunlight
    e. increased ability to run

21. The period from about 200,000 to 2.6 million years ago is known as the _____.
    a. Upper Neolithic
    b. Lower Neolithic
    c. Late Paleolithic
    d. Early Paleolithic
    e. Lower Paleolithic

22. Which of the following is **not** considered a "disease of civilization"?
    a. heart disease
    b. diabetes
    c. cancer
    d. tuberculosis
    e. high blood pressure

23. *Homo erectus* fossils have been found in all of the following locations **except** _____.
    a. India
    b. Canada
    c. China
    d. Java
    e. France

24. *H. erectus* first emerged around _____ years ago.
    a. 4.4 million
    b. 2.7 million
    c. 200,000
    d. 1.8 million
    e. 430,000

25. The controlled use of fire allowed for all of the following **except** _____.
    a. increase in the amount of potential social interaction with each other
    b. diminished hunting capacity
    c. greater nutritional value of foods
    d. softening of food, allowing the back teeth to get smaller
    e. increased control over the environment

26. The group of scientists that focus on the variation in the fossil record as evidence of numerous distinct biological species are called _____.
    a. loners
    b. groupers
    c. lumpers
    d. splitters
    e. splicers

27. The Neandertals are associated with the _____ tool-making tradition.
    a. Acheulian
    b. Oldowan
    c. Mousterian
    d. Paleocene
    e. Levallois

28. The period of the _____ tradition occurred between 40,000 and 125,000 years ago.
    a. Mousterian
    b. Oldowan
    c. Acheulian
    d. Levallois
    e. Neolithic

29. The Upper Paleolithic occurred between _____ and _____ year ago.
    a. 10,000/30,000
    b. 50,000/100,000
    c. 20,000/40,000
    d. 10,000/40,000
    e. none of the above

30. The hypothesis that also is called "Eve" hypothesis is the _____.
    a. multiregional hypothesis
    b. recent African origins hypothesis
    c. diffusion hypothesis
    d. African hypothesis
    e. discovery hypothesis

31. A subgroup within a species is called a(n) _____.
    a. race
    b. analogy
    c. classification
    d. attribute
    e. superspecies

32. Vitamin D is vital for maintaining the balance of _____ in the body.
    a. calcium
    b. melanin
    c. blood
    d. selenium
    e. iron

True/False Practice Questions

1. Evolution is the principle by which individuals who have the best characteristics survive to reproduce.
   True or False

2. Adaptation is the source of biological variation that gives organisms a reproductive edge.
   True or False

3. Humans are one of 10 million species on earth.
   True or False

4. Gorillas were not recognized as a species separate from humans until 1847.
   True or False

5. Only humans have binocular stereoscopic color vision.
   True or False

6. In monkeys, apes, and humans the cerebral hemispheres of the brain completely cover the cerebellum.
   True or False

7. On the whole, bonobo females form stronger bonds with one another than do chimpanzee females.
   True or False

8. Kinji Imanishi studied reconciliation among bonobos.
   True or False

9. Chimpanzees frequently use genito-genital rubbing as a way of reconciling with each other following conflict.
   True or False

10. Jane Goodall was the first known primatologist.
    True or False

11. Chimpanzees engage in perpetual sexual activity, regardless of the receptiveness of females.
    True or False

12. The hallmark of being human is bipedalism.
    True or False

13. The Oldowan tool tradition consists of hand axes, polished projectile points, and scrapers.
    True or False

14. The Mousterian tool tradition was found between 40,000 and 125.000 years ago.
    True or False

15. Human bipeds stand with one foot in nature and one in culture.
    True or False

Practice Matching

1. _____ *Homo troglodytes*

2. _____ *Homo sylvestris*

3. _____ *Australopithecus*

4. _____ *Homo habilis*

5. _____ *Homo erectus*

a. classification of human species from 1698

b. appears 2.5 million years ago

c. classification of human species by Carolus Linnaeus in 1758

d. appears less than 2 million years ago

e. earliest fossils date back 4.2 million years

Short Answer

1. What is the distinction between natural selection and adaptation?

2. Who was Carolus Linneaus?

3. What is a species?

4. Describe the evolutionary changes that occurred in primate dentition.

5. What is binocular stereoscopic color vision?

6. How do bonobos reconcile following moments of social conflict within the community?

7. Why do chimpanzees hunt?

8. Describe the differences in sexual activity among chimpanzees and bonobos.

9. Who is Kinji Imanishi and what are his contributions to primatology?

10. What are the primary characteristics of *Australopithecus*?

11. What are the adaptive changes that occurred with bipedalism?

12. What are "diseases of civilization"?

13. What evolutionary advantages occur as a result of controlling fire?

14. Who are the Neandertals and why is their a controversy about them?

15. Define race.

Practice Essays

1. How does evolution work through adaptation?

2. Describe the early attempts at human classification.

3. Why are humans classified as a primate?

4. Describe the primary evolutionary trends and tendencies among the primates.

5. What is the role of hunting within the chimpanzee community?

6. How is childhood development different between chimpanzees and bonobos?

7. What is the role of tool-making in human evolution?

8. What is the relationship between locomotive patterns and environmental adaptation?

9. How did meat-eating contribute to human evolution?

10. What were the migratory patterns of *Homo erectus*?

11. Discuss the Neandertal controversy. What are the causes of this disagreement and why is it a significant debate in our understanding of human evolution?

12. Compare and contrast the recent African origins hypothesis and the multiregional hypothesis.

13. How is race used as a marker of distinction among humans?

14. Why is race considered a sociocultural construction and not a biological truth?

Solutions

Fill-in-the-Blank

1. Primatologists
2. paleoanthropologist
3. cultural adaptation
4. primate
5. species
6. binocular stereoscopic vision
7. bonobos
8. bipedalism
9. Lower Paleolithic
10. *Homo erectus*
11. Mousterian
12. recent African origins hypothesis

Multiple-Choice Practice Questions

1. C
2. D
3. C
4. E
5. C
6. A
7. D
8. C
9. E
10. D
11. B
12. C
13. D
14. B
15. C
16. C
17. B
18. C
19. A
20. E
21. E
22. D
23. B
24. D
25. B
26. D
27. C
28. A
29. D
30. B
31. A
32. A

True/False Practice Questions

1. F
2. F
3. T
4. T
5. F
6. T
7. T
8. F
9. F
10. F
11. F
12. T
13. F
14. T
15. T

Practice Matching

1. C
2. A
3. E
4. B
5. D

Chapter 5

Language and Communication

Synopsis

Challenge Issues: What is language? How is language related to culture? How do languages change? This chapter introduces the field of anthropological linguistics, considering how existing languages are described and studied and what the history of language can tell us. The three main branches of linguistics—descriptive linguistics, historical linguistics, and language in relation to social and cultural settings—are each examined as different approaches to the study of language. In addition, this chapter explores the deeper roots of human language, from the gesture-call system to the origins of a uniquely human language and, eventually, to a writing system of visible or tactile signs.

Chapter Objectives

   I.   linguistic research and the nature of language

  II.   descriptive linguistics

 III.   historical linguistics

  IV.   language in its cultural and social settings

   V.   language versatility

  VI.   the gesture-call system

 VII.   tonal languages

VIII.   the origins of language

  IX.   from speech to writing

Key Terms

alphabet
code switching
core vocabularies
dialects
displacement
ethnolinguistics
gendered speech
gesture
glottochronology
grammar
kinesics
language
language family
linguistics
linguistic determinism

linguistic divergence
linguistic nationalism
linguistic relativity
morpheme
morphology
paralanguage
phoneme
phonetics
phonology
proxemics
signal
sociolinguistics
syntax
tonal language
writing system

Exercises

The Anthropology Resource Center (ARC)

The Anthropology Resource Center is a dynamic, subfield-specific website that provides a wealth of materials for both students and instructors to reinforce key concepts in anthropology. All of the resources and activities encourage students to apply anthropology beyond the textbook and classroom. ARC can be reached through the weblink http://thomsonedu.com/. After selecting the discipline of "Anthropology" under "Humanities and Social Sciences," go directly to ARC for a wide range of resources that bring anthropology to life through pictures, interviews, news items, interactive displays, maps, and more. (This site is passcode-protected for both instructors and students.)

Review Questions

1. Why is language so important to culture?

2. What is the anatomical "price we pay" for our vocal capabilities?

3. What have ape studies taught us about human language?

4. Distinguish between a morpheme and a phoneme and give an example of each.

5. Distinguish between grammar and syntax.

6. What is the function of substitution frames?

7. What is the purpose of a form class?

8. What method does descriptive linguistics use?

9. What is paralanguage? Provide examples.

10. What are the characteristic differences in body posture between men and women?

11. What is the "gesture-call" system?

12. What is the biology of human speech?

13. Describe the Sapir-Whorf Hypothesis.

14. What are social dialects?

15. What is code switching? Give an example that you have observed.

16. What does glottochronology seek to explain?

17. Describe the importance of language for group identity.

18. What does ethnolinguistics seek to explain?

19. Provide an example that would support the theory of linguistic relativity.

20. What is a tonal language?

21. Why is the phenomenon of displacement important to study?

22. Why do linguists study kinship terms?

23. Your text notes that wild speculation about the origins of language is no longer necessary. What advances have been made that make such speculation unnecessary?

24. What types of communication have primates been taught?

25. What are the communicative capabilities of monkeys and apes?

26. What is the difference between a signal and a symbol?

Fill-in-the-Blank

1. The central and most highly developed human system of communication is _____.

2. A symbol has an arbitrary meaning determined by cultural convention, while a _____ has a natural or self-evident meaning.

3. Of all the potential sounds that can be made by the human vocal system, no more than _____ are used by any particular language.

4. The modern scientific study of language by Europeans began in the _____ with the collection of information about exotic languages by European explorers, invaders, and missionaries.

5. _____ is the systematic study of the production, transmission, and reception of speech sounds.

6. The smallest class of sound that makes a difference in meaning is called a _____.

7. The smallest significant unit of sound that carries a meaning is called a _____.

8. The entire formal structure of a language is called its _____.

9. Pronouns, lower numerals, and names for body parts and natural objects for the _____ of languages.

10. _____ refers to the extralinguistic noises that accompany language.

11. A series of symbols representing the sounds of a language is called a(n) _____

12. Today some _____ people claim English as their native language.

13. _____ is usually referred to as "body language."

14. _____ linguistics studies relationships between earlier and later languages.

15. English belongs to the _____ language family.

16. Linguistic _____ refers to the attempt by nations to proclaim their independence and distinctive identity by celebrating their own language.

17. The study of the relationship between language and social factors is called _____.

18. The process by which a person changes from one level of language to another is called _____.

Multiple-Choice Practice Questions

1. A system of communication based on symbols is called a _____.
   a. signal
   b. substitution frame
   c. language
   d. form class
   e. vocalization

2. All languages are organized on the same basic plan in that _____.
   a. they are all based on signals
   b. they take no more than fifty sounds and put them together in meaningful ways according to rules that can be determined by linguists.
   c. they take no more than three thousand sounds and organize them according to the rules of grammar
   d. they all evolved from a common Egyptian language
   e. they originated in Russia

3. The modern scientific study of all aspects of language is _____.
   a. kinesics
   b. phonology
   c. linguistics
   d. grammar
   e. glottochronology

4. The systematic study of the production, transmission, and reception of speech sounds is _____.
   a. linguistics
   b. morphology
   c. frame substitution
   d. phonetics
   e. syntax

5. Paralanguage is to speech as _____ is to position of the body.
   a. kinesics
   b. ethnolinguistics
   c. form class
   d. phonetics
   e. displacement

6. Consider the English word "dog." Which of the following is a morpheme?
   a. "d"
   b. "dog"
   c. "o"
   d. "g"
   e. "d," "dog," "o," and "g"

7. Which of the following is not part of the same substation frame in English?
   a. house
   b. cat
   c. daisy
   d. think
   e. car

8. Which of the following contains the human vocal chords?
   a. palate
   b. trachea
   c. epiglottis

d. pharynx

e. larynx

9. Which the following is **not** a Latin-based language?

   a. Spanish

   b. Romanian

   c. German

   d. Italian

   e. Portuguese

10. Kinesics is a method for notating and analyzing _____.

    a. screaming

    b. kissing

    c. any form of body 'language.'

    d. fighting

    e. food

11. Descriptive linguistics _____.

    a. attempts to explain the features of a particular language at one time in its history

    b. looks at languages as separate systems without considering how they might be related to each other

    c. attempts to construct a language's historical development

    d. investigates relationships between earlier and later forms of the same language

    e. "attempts to explain the features of a particular language at one time in its history" and "looks at languages as separate systems without considering how they might be related to each other"

12. A language family is a group of languages that _____.

    a. all have the same core vocabulary

    b. are subordinate to a dominant language

    c. all have the same syntax

    d. use the same number of sounds

    e. are descended from a single ancestral language

13. If the core vocabulary of two languages is compared by glottochronologists, it is thought possible to determine _____.

    a. if the two languages perceive reality in the same way

    b. if the two languages use the same syntax

    c. if they share the same allophones

    d. if they have a similar technology

    e. how long ago the languages separated from each other

14. Which of the following statements about linguistic divergence is **incorrect**?
    a. One force for linguistic change is borrowing by one language from another.
    b. If languages were isolated from each other, there would be very little linguistic change.
    c. New vocabulary emerges in a language due to quest for novelty and the development of specialized vocabulary by groups.
    d. Changes in pronunciation may emerge as markers of class boundary (e.g., upper-class"U" versus "Non-U").
    e. Dying languages may be revived in the name of linguistic nationalism.

15. Which of the following is **not** an example of linguistic nationalism?
    a. You are a Spanish-speaking person in the United States and want your children to learn English, so that they can assimilate more completely into the society around them.
    b. A national committee in France declares that certain widely used terms will no longer be allowed to appear in public print because they are not French.
    c. You live in Scotland and are so alarmed by the rapid decline in the number of people speaking Gaelic that you start a school in which all subjects are taught in Gaelic.
    d. The southern part of India declares itself a separate country called Tamiland (the land of the people who speak Tamil) in defiance of India's declaration of Hindi as the national language; people say they will die in defense of their "mother tongue."
    e. A country previously colonized by the British passes a law requiring everyone to speak the native tongue; English is banned because of its association with colonial domination.

16. The influence of a person's class status on what pronunciation he/she uses; a speaker's choice of more complicated vocabulary and grammar when he/she is speaking to a professional audience; the influence of language on culture-all these are the concerns of _____.
    a. descriptive linguistics
    b. historical linguistics
    c. ethnolinguistics
    d. linguistic nationalism
    e. displacement

17. Which of the following statements about the theory of linguistic relativity is **incorrect**?
    a. It was first formulated by Edward Sapir and Benjamin Whorf
    b. It may be briefly explained with the sentence, "Language determines the reality that speakers of the language perceive."
    c. It may be briefly explained with the sentence, "Language reflects reality; it only mirrors what people perceive."
    d. It is expressed in this example: If in a factory a metal drum is labeled "empty" (when in fact it is filled with flammable fumes), people will perceive it as empty and may do things with it that may create a fire hazard (such as storing it near a furnace); but if it is labeled "full" of gaseous fumes, people will perceive it as a fire hazard and treat it more carefully
    e. none of these are incorrect

18. The term _____ is usually used to refer to varying forms of a language that reflect particular regions or social classes and that are similar enough to be mutually intelligible.

    a. dialect

    b. language subgroup

    c. language family

    d. linguistic nationalism

    e. linguistic relativity

19. On April 10, 1984, the _____ became the first community of Native Americans in the United States to affirm the right of its members to regain and maintain fluency in the ancestral language.

    a. Southern Paiute

    b. Northern Paiute

    c. Northern Ute

    d. Isleta Pueblo

    e. Apache

20. The very names for this dialect reflect the diversity of views. Which of the following are **not** terms used to refer to Ebonics.

    a. African American English (AAE)

    b. African American Vernacular (AAVE)

    c. Black English (BE)

    d. African American Dialect (AAD)

    e. they are all terms that refer to Ebonics

21. Which of the following is **not** true of Black English?

    a. It has a short history.

    b. It has logical rules of grammar.

    c. Its discourse practices cannot be traced.

    d. It has an oral literature worthy of respect.

    e. "It has a short history" and "Its discourse practices cannot be traced."

22. A specialty within linguistic anthropology that has become almost a separate field of inquiry is _____.

    a. sociolinguistics

    b. historical linguistics

    c. ethnolinguistics

    d. descriptive linguistics

    e. kinesics

23. The ability to comprehend two languages but express oneself in only one is known as receptive or _____ bilingualism.
    a. proxemic
    b. native
    c. displaced
    d. aggressive
    e. passive

24. Although we are genetically programmed to speak, what we speak is determined by our _____.
    a. parents
    b. teachers
    c. linguists
    d. culture
    e. genetic make-up

25. The first step in studying any language, once a number of utterances have been collected, is to isolate the _____.
    a. verbs
    b. nouns
    c. phonemes
    d. adjectives
    e. adverbs

26. One of the strengths of modern descriptive linguistics is the _____ of its methods.
    a. subjectivity
    b. clarity
    c. objectivity
    d. simplicity
    e. consistency

27. In North America scratching one's scalp, biting one's lip, or knitting one's brows are ways of conveying doubt. They are also what linguists call _____.
    a. morphology
    b. phonology
    c. sociolinguistic
    d. kinesics
    e. sign language

28. This approach concentrates on the way languages function now, as if they were separate systems, consistent within themselves, without any reference to historical reasons for their development.
    a. descriptive linguistics
    b. glottochronology

c. diachronic linguistics

d. historical linguistics

e. phonology

29. _____ proposed that a language is not simply an encoding process for voicing our ideas and needs but, rather, is a shaping force, which, by providing habitual grooves of expression that predispose people to see the world in a certain way, guides their thinking and behavior.

a. Benjamin Lee Whorf

b. Noah Chomsky

c. Paul Bohannan

d. Emile Durkheim

e. Robbins Burling

30. This branch of linguistics involves unraveling a language by recording, describing, and analyzing all of its features.

a. Social

b. Descriptive

c. Historical

d. Biographical

e. Phonetical

31. At least _____ percent of our total communication takes place nonverbally.

a. 25

b. 75

c. 15

d. 40

e. 60

32. The cross-cultural study of humankind's perception and use of space, came to the fore through the work of anthropologist _____.

a. Edward Hall

b. Benjamin B. Whorf

c. Alessandro Duranti

d. Gary B. Palmer

e. George Urioste

33. Specialists in this branch of linguistics investigate relationships between earlier and later forms of the same language, older languages for developments in modern ones, and questions of relationships among older language.

a. Descriptive

b. Social

c. Historical

d. Phonetic

e. Proxemics

34. When a person has the ability to comprehend two languages, but expresses herself/himself in only one, is known as _____ bilingualism.
    a. negative
    b. positive
    c. true
    d. false
    e. passive

35. It has been suggested that the alphabet was invented about _____ years ago by Semitic-speaking peoples.
    a. 4,000
    b. 2,000
    c. 10,500
    d. 7,500
    e. 3,200

36. It has been nearly 5,000 years since literacy emerged in Egypt and Iraq. Yet, today more than _____ million adults worldwide are illiterate.
    a. 25
    b. 970
    c. 550
    d. 860
    e. 75

True/False Practice Questions

1. Your text traces linguistics back to the ancient grammarians in China more than three thousand years ago.
   True or False

2. Glottochronology assumes that the rate at which a language's core vocabulary changes is variable and thus cannot be used to give an exact date for when two languages diverged.
   True or False

3. Human culture as we know it could have easily existed without language.
   True or False

4. Though men and women in North American culture typically utilize slightly different vocabularies, the body language they use does not differ much.
   True or False

5. The emphasis on the French language by Quebecois separatists is an example of linguistic nationalism.
   True or False

6. "Ebonics" is a substandard or defective dialect of English.
   True or False

7. The chimpanzee Chantek learned English as well as American Sign Language.
   True or False

8. Detailed knowledge of a culture's language is essential to a full understanding of the culture.
   True or False

9. Linguistics has five main branches of study.
   True or False

10. The study of language sounds is called morphology.
    True or False

11. The overlapping routes of passage for food and air can be seen as a legacy of human evolutionary history.
    True or False

12. The English language uses no definite articles.
    True or False

13. The Spanish spoken by Tarascan Indians in Mexico is a result of colonialism.
    True or False

14. 10% of the global population speaks English as a native language.
    True or False

15. 80% of today's internet users are speakers of just 10 of the world's 6500 languages.
    True or False

16. The Northern Ute Indians have reclaimed their indigenous language.
    True or False

17. The idea that distinctions encoded in one language are unique to that language is called linguistic relativity.
    True or False

18. No language uses more than about 100 sounds to communicate.
    True or False

19. Human language is always embedded within a gesture-call system of a type we share with monkeys and apes.
    True or False

20. Cross-cultural research has shown few similarities around the world for such basic facial expressions as smiling, laughing, crying, and variations of anger.
    True or False

21. Like Spanish, English distinguishes between feminine and masculine nouns.
    True or False

22. By applying a logarithmic formula to two related core vocabularies, one can determine how many years two languages have been separated.
    True or False

Practice Matching

Match the term to its definition.

1. _____ morpheme
2. _____ phonemes
3. _____ form classes
4. _____ kinesics
5. _____ glottochronology

a. A method of dating divergence within language families.
b. The smallest classes of sound that make a difference in meaning.
c. The smallest unit of sound that carries meaning.
d. Postures, facial expressions, and body motion.
e. The parts of speech that work the same in any sentence.

Practice Short Answer

1. Identify the branches of the science of linguistics.

2. What is a morpheme? Define and provide an example.

3. What accounts for the universality of various cries and facial expressions, as well as for the great difficulty people have in bluffing or especially lying through gesture-calls?

4. Explain why Mandarin Chinese is considered a tonal language and English is not.

5. Among other things, the way a person stands often reveals something about his or her gender. Provide examples to support this observation.

6. Provide an example of a language that uses gendered speech and explain why it is considered gendered speech.

Practice Essays

1. Would it be accurate to claim language as a distinguishing feature of *H. sapiens*? Why or why not? What evidence exists for the uniqueness or non-uniqueness of human language?

2. How is language linked to gender? Use examples from the text and add some of your own.

3. What was the Northern Ute Language Renewal Project?

4. Of central importance to the development of human culture is language. How might language have started in the first place?

5. What is the theory of linguistic relativity? What do its detractors say about it?

6. Gender language reveals how women and men relate to each other. Exactly what does it reveal about how women and men relate?

7. Perhaps the most powerful force for linguistic change is the domination of one society over another. Provide examples of linguistic change brought about by colonialism.

8. Discuss Project Chantek and its findings.

9. Although thousands of languages have existed only in spoken form, many have long been documented in one form or writing or another. Discuss the emergence and development of writing systems.

Solutions

Fill-in-the-Blank

1. language
2. signal
3. 50
4. 1500s
5. Phonetics
6. phoneme
7. morpheme
8. grammar
9. core vocabulary
10. Paralanguage
11. alphabet
12. 375 million
13. Kinesics
14. Historical
15. Indo-European
16. nationalism
17. sociolinguistics
18. code switching

Multiple-Choice Practice Questions

1. C
2. B
3. C
4. D
5. A
6. B
7. D
8. E
9. C
10. C
11. E
12. E
13. E
14. B
15. A
16. C
17. C
18. A
19. C
20. D
21. E
22. C
23. E
24. D
25. C
26. C
27. D
28. A
29. A
30. B
31. E
32. A
33. C
34. E
35. A
36. D

True/False Practice Questions

1. F
2. F
3. T
4. F
5. T
6. F
7. F
8. T
9. F
10. F
11. T
12. F
13. T
14. F
15. T
16. T
17. T
18. F
19. T
20. F
21. F
22. T

Practice Matching

1. C
2. B
3. E
4. D
5. A

Chapter 6

Social Identity, Personality, and Gender

Synopsis

Challenge Issues: What is enculturation? How does enculturation influence personality? Are different personalities characteristic of different cultures? This chapter focuses on how culture is transmitted from one generation to the next and explores the cultural contexts in which personalities are formed. Examining both biological and cultural data, the chapter introduces concepts of alternative genders and suggests a relativistic understanding of normality and abnormality.

Chapter Objectives

    I.   enculturation: the human self and social identity

   II.   personality

  III.   alternative gender models from a cross-cultural perspective

  IV.   normal and abnormal personality in social context

Key Terms

core values
dependence training
ethnic psychosis
independence training
intersexual

modal personality
naming ceremony
personality
self-awareness
transgender

Exercises

The Anthropology Resource Center (ARC)

The Anthropology Resource Center is a dynamic, subfield-specific website that provides a wealth of materials for both students and instructors to reinforce key concepts in anthropology. All of the resources and activities encourage students to apply anthropology beyond the textbook and classroom. ARC can be reached through the weblink http://thomsonedu.com/. After selecting the discipline of "Anthropology" under "Humanities and Social Sciences," go directly to ARC for a wide range of resources that bring anthropology to life through pictures, interviews, news items, interactive displays, maps, and more. (This site is passcode-protected for both instructors and students.)

Review Questions

1. Who are the agents of enculturation?

2. What are the four basic orientations of self-awareness?

3. Why might North American children's motor development lag behind that of children from non-Western societies?

4. What is personality and how does it develop?

5. Describe the significance of the naming ceremony.

6. Describe the development of personality among the Ju/'hoansi.

7. It was stated that what has seemed to be "normal" in the past, could become "abnormal" in the future. And conversely, it is also true that the abnormal may become the normal. What is meant by these statements?

8. Distinguish between dependence and independence training.

9. What did Margaret Mead's study of adolescent Samoans tell us?

10. Provide an example of modal personality.

11. Explain the basic statistics behind the concept of modal personality.

12. What purpose do the Rorschach and Thematic Appreception Tests serve?

13. What is "core values"? Provide examples.

14. Who were the "castrati" and what social role did they serve?

15. What contribution did Ruth Benedict make to the field of culture-and-personality?

16. Why were national character studies undertaken? What were the major objections to national character studies?

17. Distinguish between the terms intersexual and transgender.

18. Who were the "sadhus" and what was their importance?

19. What is the anthropological approach to mental illness?

20. What is the function of the *two-spirit* in Plains Indians society?

21. Give examples of ethnic psychoses.

22. How is abnormal behavior defined?

23. What factors may cause a change in the perception of mental illnesses?

24. What is "windigo?"

Fill-in-the-Blank

1. The Enlightenment thinker John Locke presented the concept of _____ to express the idea that humans are born as "blank slates" and that everything depends on experience.

2. The term _____ refers to the process by which culture is transmitted from one generation to the next.

3. The ability to get from one object or place to another is called _____.

4. Margaret Mead studied three societies in _____ and found out that sex roles were highly variable.

5. Margaret Mead was a founder of the field called _____.

6. The Ju/'hoansi made a living by _____ in the Kalahari Desert.

7. A concept that attempted to retain the idea of a group personality and yet take into account the diversity of personalities within a group is the concept of _____.

8. The ink-blot test is properly called the _____ test.

9. The studies developed during World War II to explore the idea that modern nations could be characterized by personality types were called _____ studies.

10. The psychosis exhibited by northern Algonquian Indian groups who recognize the existence of cannibalistic monsters is called _____.

Multiple-Choice Practice Questions

1. Enculturation is the process of transmitting _____.
   a. society from one generation to the next
   b. social norms from one adult to another
   c. culture from one child to another
   d. culture from one generation to the next
   e. personality from parent to child

2. The agents of enculturation _____.
   a. are persons involved in transmitting culture to the next generation
   b. are at first the members of the family into which the child is born
   c. vary, depending on the structure of the family into which a child is born
   d. include peer groups and schoolteachers
   e. "are persons involved in transmitting culture to the next generation", "are at first the members of the family into which the child is born", "vary, depending on the structure of the family into which a child is born" and "include peer groups and schoolteachers"

3. Which of the following statements about self-awareness is **incorrect**?
   a. Self-awareness occurs earlier in children as a function of the amount of social stimulation they receive.
   b. At fifteen weeks of age, the home-reared infant in North America is in contact with its mother for about 20 percent of time.
   c. At fifteen weeks of age, infants in Ju/'hoansi society are in close contact with their mothers about 70 percent of the time.

d. American children develop self-awareness earlier than do Ju/'hoansi children.

e. "Self-awareness occurs earlier in children as a function of the amount of social stimulation they receive", "At fifteen weeks of age, the home-reared infant in North America is in contact with its mother for about 20 percent of time", "At fifteen weeks of age, infants in the Ju/'hoansi society of South Africa's Kalahari Desert are in close contact with their mothers about 70 percent of the time" and "American children develop self-awareness earlier than do Ju/'hoansi children."

4. The _____ includes definitions and explanations of objects, spatial orientation, and temporal orientation, as well as culturally defined values, ideals, and standards that provide an individual with a normative orientation.

   a. vital self

   b. *tabula rasa*

   c. behavioral environment

   d. patterns of affect

   e. core values

5. In studying three societies in New Guinea, Margaret Mead found that the role played by men and women were determined primarily by _____.

   a. genes

   b. biology

   c. culture

   d. incest

   e. the food they ate

6. Margaret Mead's groundbreaking work in culture and personality published in 1928 was a deliberate test of a Western psychological hypothesis. What was this hypothesis?

   a. Lowering the drinking age will promote promiscuity.

   b. Child-rearing practices have no effect on adult personality.

   c. The stress and conflict experienced by American adolescents is a universal phenomenon based on maturing hormones.

   d. By changing child-rearing practices, we can change the structure of society.

   e. By lowering the driving age, we can promote less stress among adolescents.

7. A study of child rearing among the Ju/'hoansi of Africa indicates that _____.

   a. boys and girls are raised in a very similar manner and are both mild-mannered and self-reliant

   b. because girls are out gathering most of the time, they are expected to be more aggressive and self-reliant than boys are

   c. mothers spend the least amount of time with their children, and thus the children identify strongly with their fathers

   d. boys do more work than girls

   e. boys have less responsibility than girls and get to play more of the time

8. Independence training is more likely in _____.
   a. small nuclear families
   b. large extended families
   c. small-scale horticultural societies where a man has many wives
   d. a pastoralist family where a woman has many husbands and the extended family has to be always on the move
   e. New York City neighborhoods where large families stay nearby

9. Dependence training is more likely in _____.
   a. nuclear families
   b. societies whose subsistence is based on pastoralism
   c. a food-foraging society
   d. extended families in societies whose economy is based on subsistence farming
   e. industrial societies

10. The personality typical of a society, as indicated by the central tendency of a defined frequency distribution, is called _____.
    a. core values
    b. nuclear personality
    c. patterns of affect
    d. culture and personality
    e. modal personality

11. Which of the following statements about modal personality is correct?
    a. Although a modal personality may be found for a particular society, a range of personalities may exist in that society.
    b. Although the modal personality may be considered "normal" for that society, it may be shared by less than half of the population.
    c. Those who study modal personality accept the fact that there may be abnormal individuals in that society.
    d. Data on modal personality are usually gathered by the use of psychological tests such as the Rorschach and TAT.
    e. "Although a modal personality may be found for a particular society, a range of personalities may exist in that society", "Although the modal personality may be considered "normal" for that society, it may be shared by less than half of the population", "Those who study modal personality accept the fact that there may be abnormal individuals in that society" and "Data on modal personality are usually gathered by the use of psychological tests such as the Rorschach and TAT."

12. Studies of _____ were developed during World War II to explore the idea that basic personality traits were shared by most of the people in modern nations.
    a. modal personality
    b. national character

c. stereotype

d. group personality

e. independence training

13. The term "core values" refers to _____.

    a. those aspects of culture that pertain to the way a culture makes its living

    b. rules that guide family and home life

    c. those values emphasized by a particular culture

    d. common shares in Golden Delicious Corp

    e. the beliefs stressed by a particular political party

14. Among the Plains Indians, a man who wore women's clothes, performed women's work, and married another man _____.

    a. was considered normal

    b. was sought out as a curer, artist, and matchmaker

    c. was assumed to have great spiritual power

    d. might have been homosexual

    e. "was considered normal", "was sought out as a curer, artist, and matchmaker", "was assumed to have great spiritual power" and "might have been homosexual"

15. An ethnic psychosis refers to a _____.

    a. psychotic episode experienced by a person from an exotic culture

    b. progressive disease that strikes anthropologists when they spend more than twelve months in the field

    c. psychosis characterized by symptoms peculiar to a particular group

    d. universal form of mental illness

    e. biologically based disease that resembles schizophrenia

16. Traditional culture and personality studies _____.

    a. were important in undermining ethnocentrism

    b. are criticized today for being impressionistic and difficult to replicate

    c. diversified the study of psychological processes in a cultural context

    d. promoted a relativistic point of view

    e. "were important in undermining ethnocentrism", "are criticized today for being impressionistic and difficult to replicate", "diversified the study of psychological processes in a cultural context" and "promoted a relativistic point of view"

17. According to your textbook, among the Yanomami _____.

    a. all men are fierce and warlike

    b. all men are quiet and retiring

    c. there is a range of personalities

    d. a quiet, retiring Yanomamo would not survive

    e. a fierce, warlike Yanomamo would not survive

18. In _____ infants generally do not sleep with their parents, most often being put in rooms of their own. This is seen as an important step in making them into individuals, "owners" of themselves and their capacities, rather than part of some social whole.

    a. the Ituri rain forest

    b. China

    c. the United States

    d. Mexico

    e. the Kalahari Desert

19. As _____ pioneering studies suggested, whatever biological differences may exist between men and women, they are extremely malleable.

    a. Ruth Benedict's

    b. Karen Sacks's

    c. Deborah Tannen's

    d. Margaret Mead's

    e. Laura Nader's

20. One of the "founding mothers" of anthropology is _____.

    a. Nancy Scheper-Hughes

    b. Catherine Bateson

    c. Mary Douglas

    d. Margaret Mead

    e. Emily Schultz

21. Today in Native American societies the preferred term to describe an individual who falls between the categories of "man" and "woman" is known as _____.

    a. berdache

    b. gay

    c. passive homosexual

    d. two-spirit

    e. effeminate

22. We should not be surprised to find that explanations of the universe are never entirely objective in nature, but are _____.

    a. culturally constructed

    b. figments of one's imagination

    c. scientifically constructed

    d. evolved historically

    e. simply absurd

23. Usually regarded as dreaded liabilities, anthropologist _____ suggests that, in North America, aspects of manic-depression and Attention Deficit Hyperactivity Disorder (ADHD) are coming to be seen as assets in the quest for success.

    a. Jennifer Thompson

b. Vicki Cassman

c. Emily Martin

d. Martha Knack

e. William Jankowiak

24. All societies must somehow ensure that their culture is adequately transmitted from one generation to the next. This transmission process is _____.

a. acculturation

b. assimilation

c. enculturation

d. absorption

e. integration

25. Which of the following is **not** associated with the development of self-awareness?

a. spatial orientation

b. temporal orientation

c. normative orientation

d. behavioral orientation

e. object orientation

26. The _____ personality is the personality typical of a society as indicated by the central tendency of a defined frequency distribution.

a. normal

b. average

c. standard

d. mean

e. modal

27. Data on modal personality are best gathered with psychological tests administered to a sample of the population in question. Those most often used would include which of the following?

a. SAT

b. Rorschach, or inkblot test

c. DAP (Draw a Person Test)

d. TAT (Thematic Apperception Test)

e. Rorschach, or inkblot test and TAT (Thematic Apperception Test)

28. Ruth Benedict studied each of the following cultural groups except _____.

a. Aymara

b. Melanesians

c. Kwakiutl

d. Dobu

e. Zuni

29. _____ is a fear reaction often occurring in middle-aged Malay women of low intelligence who are subservient and self-effacing.
    a. Koro
    b. Saka
    c. Windigo
    d. Pibloktoq
    e. Latah

30. Among the _____, a child was first introduced to the joy of community in the First Laugh Ceremony.
    a. Icelanders
    b. Aymara Indians
    c. Hopi
    d. Netsilik Inuit
    e. Navajo

31. _____ orientation includes standards that indicate what ranges of behavior are acceptable for males and females in a particular society.
    a. Spatial
    b. Temporal
    c. Normative
    d. Objective
    e. Gender

True/False Practice Questions

1. What is considered "normal" in a society is defined by culture.
   True or False

2. Anthropologists believe that all mental illness is learned rather than biologically based.
   True or False

3. Both hunting and gathering societies and industrial societies promote independence training in their mobile nuclear families.
   True or False

4. Margaret Mead believed that male and female roles were by and large defined by the biological attributes of the sexes.
   True or False

5. National character studies developed during World War II to explore the idea that basic personality traits were shared by most of the people in modern nations.
   True or False

6. Dependence and independence training are completely different and are not part of a continuum of behavior.
   True or False

7. The Yanomami of Brazil are known for their "fierceness," yet there is a range of personality types even there.
   True or False

8. The Native American view sees intersexed individuals in a positive and affirming light.
   True or False

9. The Euro-American view of intersexed individuals is similar to the Native American view.
   True or False

10. The extent to which Native Americans see spirituality is reflected in their belief that all things have spirit.
    True or False

11. Gender bending is culturally very rare.
    True or False

12. True hermaphrodites have both testicular and ovarian tissue.
    True or False

13. In the United States in 2000, some 8.5% of all cohabiting couples were unmarried.
    True or False

14. Core values never change within a culture.
    True or False

15. What was abnormal in the past may become normal.
    True or False

16. Today, for a man to assume a feminine identity is not regarded as abnormal by European-Americans; in fact, such individuals are regarded as special in that they bridge the gap between the purely feminine and purely masculine.
    True or False

17. In food-foraging societies child-rearing practices combine elements of both dependence and independence training.
    True or False

18. As hard as they have tried, anthropologists have never found a quiet and retiring Yanomami man.
    True or False

19. What defines normal behavior in any culture is determined by the culture itself, and what may be acceptable, or even admirable, in one may not be in another.
    True or False

20. Breast-feeding tends to be relatively long-lived in the industrialized world, due to workplace conditions which facilitate it.
    True or False

21. It has become clear that each culture provides different opportunities and has different expectations for ideal or acceptable male-female behavior.
    True or False

22. Clearly, the biological capacity for what we think of as humanhood, which entails culture, must be nurtured to be realized.
    True or False

Short Answer Practice Questions

1. Describe the Navajo naming ceremony

2. Compare and contrast self-awareness and personality.

3. What is a modal personality? Provide an example.

4. What are the most important aspects in personality development?

5. Common sense suggests that personalities appropriate for one culture may be less appropriate for others. Provide examples that would support this statement.

Practice Essays

1. It was stated that what has seemed to be "normal" in the past, could become "abnormal" in the future. And conversely, it is also true that the abnormal may become the normal. What is meant by these statements? Provide examples.

2. Compare and contrast a modal personality with a group personality.

3. Explain how national character studies are distinct from national stereotyping that we so often do today.

4. The author of the original study The Blessed Curse mentioned, "from a very early age I was presented with two different and conflicting views of myself." What did the author mean by this? Explain.

5. Explain why the Native American and Euro-American views on intersexuality are so diametrically opposed.

6. Discuss the importance of child-rearing practices for the development of gender related personality characteristics. Provide examples.

7. Explain why child-rearing practices in the United States create problems of gender identity for both sexes, although a different sort for each sex.

8. How does a culture itself induce certain kinds of psychological conflicts that have important consequences for the entire society?

9. The Original Study is entitled "The Blessed Curse: A Foot in Both Worlds." What is the explanation for this rather unusual title?

10. What is the role and significance of ethnic psychoses in society?

11. How does a society's economy help structure the way a child is brought up and how does this, influence the development of the adult personality?

12. There are people who do not fit neatly into a binary gender standard. Identify those people and explain why they do not fit neatly into a binary gender standard.

13. Describe the range of inherited and artificially imposed sexual features that human cultures have dealt with in the course of thousands of years.

Solutions

Fill-in-the-Blank

1. tabula rasa
2. enculturation
3. spatial orientation
4. New Guinea
5. Culture and Personality
6. food foraging
7. modal personality
8. Rorschach
9. national character
10. windigo

Multiple-Choice Practice Questions

1. D
2. E
3. D
4. C
5. C
6. C
7. A
8. A
9. D
10. E
11. E
12. B
13. C
14. E
15. C
16. E
17. C
18. C
19. D
20. D
21. D
22. A
23. C
24. C
25. C
26. E
27. E
28. A
29. E
30. E
31. C

True/False Practice Questions

1. T
2. F
3. T
4. F
5. T
6. F
7. T
8. T
9. F
10. T
11. F
12. T
13. T
14. F
15. T
16. F
17. T
18. F
19. T
20. F
21. T
22. T

Chapter 7

Patterns of Subsistence

Synopsis

Challenge Issues: What is adaptation? How do humans adapt culturally? What sorts of cultural adaptations have humans achieved through the ages? In this chapter the text examines the impact that various modes of subsistence have on cultures. Cultural adaptation and evolution create a dynamic interaction between organism and environment. Food-foraging and food-producing societies are described in detail, including the variations in food production systems over time.

Chapter Objectives

   I.   adaptation

  II.   modes of subsistence

 III.   food-foraging societies

  IV.   food-producing societies

   V.   industrial societies

Key Terms

agriculture
carrying capacity
convergent evolution
cultural adaptation
cultural evolution
culture area
culture core
density of social relations
ecosystem

food foraging
horticulture
Neolithic
Neolithic transition
parallel evolution
peasant
progress
slash-and-burn cultivation

Exercises

The Anthropology Resource Center (ARC)

The Anthropology Resource Center is a dynamic, subfield-specific website that provides a wealth of materials for both students and instructors to reinforce key concepts in anthropology. All of the resources and activities encourage students to apply anthropology beyond the textbook and classroom. ARC can be reached through the weblink http://thomsonedu.com/. After selecting the discipline of "Anthropology" under "Humanities and Social Sciences," go directly to ARC for a wide range of resources that bring anthropology to life through pictures, interviews, news items, interactive displays, maps, and more. (This site is passcode-protected for both instructors and students.)

Review Questions

1. What purpose does adaptation serve?

2. Describe the relationship the Tsembaga have with the environment.

3. Explain what is meant by adaptation.

4. Explain the culture core of two societies.

5. Describe Comanche adaptation to the plains environment.

6. Distinguish between convergent and parallel evolution.

7. Provide an example of how a culture can be stable while not necessarily static.

8. Discuss the findings of Ann Kendall's research.

9. Why did native groups on the plains not farm?

10. What is the role of the ethnoscientist?

11. About how many people currently live by food foraging?

12. What previously held misconceptions of food foragers have been refuted?

13. What are the main social characteristics of food foragers?

14. What are the size-limiting factors in a foraging group?

15. What purpose does population redistribution serve for the Ju/'hoansi?

16. What impact does biological sex have on the division of labor?

17. How is the behavior of food-foraging groups reflected in their material culture?

18. Why are food foragers generally egalitarian?

19. Can we make any generalizations about the status of women in foraging societies?

20. How is territory conceptualized in foraging societies?

21. What are the characteristics of agricultural societies?

22. Distinguish between horticulturalists and agriculturalists.

23. What are the basic features of pastoralist society?

24. Define "adaptation" and "ecosystem" and illustrate the relevance of these concepts with the example of pig sacrifices among the Tsembaga.

25. Why has slash-and-burn come to be viewed negatively by many people today?

26. Describe the subsistence practices of the Mekranoti.

27. Describe the characteristics of the Aztec state.

Fill-in-the-Blank

1. _____ is the process by which organisms modify and adjust to their environment and thereby survive more effectively.

2. A system composed of both the natural environment and all the organisms living in it is called the _____.

3. When the Comanche migrated to the Great Plains, they found a new food source, the _____.

4. When several societies with different cultural backgrounds move into a new environment and develop similar adaptations, they represent the cultural equivalent of _____ evolution.

5. When several societies with very similar cultural backgrounds develop along similar lines, they represent the process of _____ evolution.

6. A geographic region in which a number of different societies follow a similar pattern of life is called a culture _____.

7. Hunting, fishing, and gathering wild foods is called _____.

8. The _____ is the number and intensity of interactions among the members of a camp.

9. _____ is the seasonal movement of livestock between high altitude and lowland valleys.

10. _____ try to understand folk ideologies and how they help a group survive.

11. Humans lived using food foraging until about _____ years ago, when domestication of animals and plants began.

12. With the intensification of _____, some farming villages became urbanized.

13. The number of people who can be supported by a certain technology is the _____ of the environment.

14. About _____ percent of the diet of most food foragers is gathered by women.

15. Increased food sharing appears to be related to a shift in food habits involving increased eating of _____ around two and a half million years ago.

16. Another name for slash-and-burn is _____ farming.

17. The Bakhtiari of the Zagros Mountains are _____ who migrate seasonally from one location to another.

18. City life is based on a subsistence pattern of _____.

19. The main city of the Aztecs was _____.

20. The anthropologist who conducted her research in the Andes Mountains of southern Peru was _____.

Multiple-Choice Practice Questions

1. Adaptation refers to the _____.
   a. process by which organisms modify and adjust to their environment and thereby survive more effectively
   b. ability of one population to destroy another
   c. borrowing of cultural material from another society
   d. process by which living systems change from birth to death
   e. effect of child-rearing practices on basic personality structure

2. Before the arrival of horses and guns, the Comanche were food foragers in southern Idaho. Their skill as hunters was put to good use as they used these new tools to hunt buffalo on the Great Plains. The term used to refer to existing customs that by chance have potential for a new cultural adaptation is _____.
   a. convergent evolution
   b. divergent evolutions
   c. ecosystem
   d. parallel evolution
   e. pre-adaptations

3. The Comanche and the Cheyenne were quite different culturally until they moved out onto the Great Plains and made use of the horse to hunt buffalo and raid settled peoples. They then became more similar in cultural adaptations, a process called _____.
   a. pre-adaptation
   b. development of a culture area
   c. convergent evolution
   d. parallel evolution
   e. an ecosystem

4. Native American food foragers established a way of life in New England and southern Quebec that lasted about five thousand years. This is indicative of _____.
   a. stagnation
   b. failure to progress
   c. genetic inferiority
   d. lack of innovation
   e. effective cultural adaptation

5. A culture type is defined by _____.
   a. the geographic area in which a people live
   b. the kind of technology that a group has to exploit a particular environment
   c. contacts with other cultures
   d. sharing the same values
   e. sharing the same language

6. A taboo against eating certain foods, the belief that only a chief has strong enough magic to plant apple trees and dispense them to his fellow villagers, and the number of hours a people work each day are examples of what could be considered part of a society's _____.
   a. structural base
   b. foundation
   c. infrastructure
   d. culture core
   e. none of these

7. Which of the following research topics might be of interest to an ethnoscientist?
   a. How the allele responsible for sickle-cell anemia increases or decreases in certain cultural environments, such a horticultural vs. hunting-gathering.
   b. Similarities and differences in the farming patterns of Southwest Asia and Mesoamerica
   c. The ways in which a group classifies and explains the world; for example, the Tsembaga avoid low-lying, marshy areas filled with mosquitoes that carry malaria because they believe that such areas are inhabited by red spirits who punish trespassers
   d. Reconstruction and comparison of archaeological sites in similar geographic regions
   e. "How the allele responsible for sickle-cell anemia increases or decreases in certain cultural environments, such a horticultural vs. hunting-gathering", "Similarities and differences in the farming patterns of Southwest Asia and Mesoamerica", "The ways in which a group classifies and explains the world; for example, the Tsembaga avoid low-lying, marshy areas filled with mosquitoes that carry malaria because they believe that such areas are inhabited by red spirits who punish trespassers" and "Reconstruction and comparison of archaeological sites in similar geographic regions"

8. Some anthropologists refer to food foragers as "the original affluent society" because _____.
   a. they manage to accumulate a lot of wealth
   b. they occupy the most attractive environments with abundant food supply
   c. they live in marginal areas and are very poor
   d. they earn a good wage for all hours of work they put in each week
   e. they work only twelve to nineteen hours a week for a comfortable, healthy life

9. The groups referred to as food foragers must live where there are naturally available food sources; thus they _____.
   a. remain in permanent settlements
   b. move about once every ten years
   c. move frequently
   d. adopt farming whenever they can
   e. prefer to live in cities

10. The number and intensity of interactions among the members of a residential unit is called _____.
    a. density of social relations
    b. social interactionism

    c. cultural ecology

    d. carrying capacity

    e. convergent evolution

11. Which of the following is **not** one of the three elements of human social organization that developed with hunting?

    a. sexual division of labor

    b. aggressive behavior

    c. food sharing

    d. the camp site

    e. "sexual division of labor", "aggressive behavior", "food sharing" and "the camp site"

12. In a food-foraging society, how do people store food for the future?

    a. They keep a surplus in stone cairns.

    b. They keep extra plants in large, circular yam houses.

    c. They hide meat in each individual family residence.

    d. They rely on the generosity of others to share food.

    e. They keep dried food in a common storage shed.

13. To say that food-foraging societies are egalitarian means that _____.

    a. there are no status differences

    b. the only status differences are age and sex

    c. everyone is equal except women

    d. men are usually subordinate to women

    e. children are the center of community life

14. Someone who uses irrigation, fertilizers, and the plow to produce food on large plots of land is known as a/an _____.

    a. horticulturalist

    b. agriculturalist

    c. pastoralists

    d. hunter-gatherer

    e. industrialist

15. _____ are food producers who specialize in animal husbandry and who consider their way of life to be ideal and central to defining their identities.

    a. Food foragers

    b. Horticulturalists

    c. Agriculturalists

    d. Pastoralists

    e. Industrialists

16. Aztec society in the sixteenth century _____.
    a. was a stratified society based on achievement and education
    b. was an urbanized society in which kinship played no role in determining status
    c. was an industrial city-state
    d. was invincible to Cortes' attack
    e. none of these

17. Which of the following statements about preindustrial cities is **incorrect**?
    a. Preindustrial cities have existed in some parts of the world for thousands of years.
    b. Preindustrial cities represent a stage of development in the progression of human culture toward industrial cities.
    c. Tenochtitlan, the capital of the Aztec empire, is a good example of a preindustrial city.
    d. Preindustrial cities have a diversified economy.
    e. Preindustrial cities are highly stratified.

18. Which of the following is the oldest form of subsistence?
    a. shash-and-burn
    b. food-producing
    c. horticulture
    d. food foraging
    e. agriculture

19. After three years of tending their gardens the Mekranoti are left with only _____.
    a. manioc
    b. sweet potatoes
    c. pineapple
    d. tobacco
    e. bananas

20. A society's cultural beliefs, no matter how irrelevant they may seem to outsiders, are anything but irrelevant if one is to understand another society's _____ practices.
    a. marketing
    b. voting
    c. business
    d. trading
    e. subsistence

21. How food-foraging peoples regulate population size relates to which of the following things?
    a. how much body fat they accumulate
    b. the accumulation of material goods
    c. abortion practices

d. how they care for their children

e. "how much body fat they accumulate" and "how they care for their children"

22. Which of the following subsistence modes is based on the herding of animals?

    a. food-foraging

    b. pastoralism

    c. slash-and-burn cultivation

    d. hunting and gathering

    e. farming

23. The _____ process establishes a moving balance between the needs of a population and the potential of its environment.

    a. adaptation

    b. accommodation

    c. integration

    d. evolution

    e. adjustment

24. The kind of development where similar cultural adaptations to similar environmental conditions by peoples whose ancestral cultures were quite different is called _____.

    a. parallel evolution

    b. complementary evolution

    c. concurrent evolution

    d. affinal evolution

    e. convergent evolution

25. A(n) _____ is a rural cultivator whose surpluses are transferred to a dominant group of rulers.

    a. agriculturalist

    b. forager

    c. pastoralist

    d. horticulturalist

    e. peasant

26. The number of people the available resources can support at a given technological level is known as the _____.

    a. density of social relations

    b. equilibrium point

    c. carrying capacity

    d. point of diminishing capacity

    e. balanced position

27. Food foragers like the _____ have a division of labor in which women gather and prepare "bush" food, but hunting is usually done by men.
    a. Mekranoti
    b. Crow
    c. Ju/'hoansi
    d. Bahktiari
    e. Tutsi

28. Although we tend to think of people as either food foragers or food producers, there are numerous examples of people like the _____, who rely on a mix of wild and domesticated resources.
    a. Ju/'hoansi
    b. Comanche
    c. Aymara
    d. Bakhtiari
    e. Papago

29. Aztec agricultural success provided for which of the following?
    a. a highly mobile population
    b. an increasingly large population
    c. the diversification of labor
    d. a more egalitarian society
    e. "an increasingly large population" and "the diversification of labor"

30. Intensive agriculture, a more complex activity than swidden farming, requires which of the following?
    a. irrigation
    b. fertilizers
    c. draft animals
    d. a high level of mobility
    e. "irrigation", "fertilizers" and "draft animals"

31. A people's _____ adaptation consists of a complex of ideas, activities, and technologies that enable them to survive and even thrive.
    a. social
    b. cultural
    c. economic
    d. political
    e. religious

32. Which Native American group was part of Great Plains culture area?
    a. Iroquois
    b. Cheyenne

    c. Apache

    d. Comanche

    e. b and d

33. Muslims and Jews have a food taboo against the consumption of _____.

    a. horses

    b. cattle

    c. pigs

    d. dogs

    e. cats

34. Pastoralists are associated with which settlement pattern?

    a. urbanization

    b. semi-sedentism

    c. sedentism

    d. transhumance

    e. nomadism

35. Because the transition from food foraging to food production brought about radical transformations in every aspect of the cultural systems involved in the move, archaeologist _____ introduced the term "Neolithic revolution."

    a. Marshall Sahlins

    b. Gordon Childe

    c. Alan Simmons

    d. Franz Boas

    e. J. H. Steward

True/False Practice Questions

1. According to the Original Study, the Mekranoti had to work hard to get enough produce from their gardens.
   True or False

2. The Mbuti live in the Ituri rain forest in the Republic of the Congo.
   True or False

3. The Bakhtiari are pastoralist nomads who drive their herds throughout the Iran-Iraq border area.
   True or False

4. Many Bakhtiari are well-educated, having attended university at home or aboard.
   True or False

5. The spread of malaria was historically linked to the development of slash-and-burn horticulture.
   True or False

6. In the world today about 3 million people live by food foraging.
   True or False

7. People started shifting to food-producing ways of life about ten thousand years ago.
   True or False

8. The average work week of the Ju/'hoansi is about fifty hours.
   True or False

9. An anthropologist would probably find it difficult to define what "progress" is.
   True or False

10. The Mekranoti style of slash-and-burn farming did not grow well because animals and insects were constantly invading their gardens.
    True or False

11. Due to their reliance of slash-and-burn farming the Mekranoti need to work very hard to survive.
    True or False

12. The Mekranoti constantly weed their gardens to keep the forest from invading.
    True or False

13. Slash-and-burn agriculture, especially in the humid tropics, may be one of the best gardening techniques possible.
    True or False

14. Peasants are part of a horticultural lifestyle.
    True or False

15. Domestication resulted in the complete eradication of food foraging.
    True or False

16. The high fertility of Mekranoti garden plots comes from the soil, not from the trees that are burned there.
    True or False

17. Because of foraging animals and destructive insects, the Mekranoti could not depend on harvesting whatever they planted.
    True or False

18. The Mekranoti do not have to work very hard to survive.
    True or False

19. Among food-foraging peoples teenage pregnancies are rampant.
    True or False

20. Food foraging would certainly not be found in a rich industrial nation such as the United States.
    True or False

21. Among food foragers today, the work of women is no less arduous than that of men.
    True or False

22. There are no sources of status differences among food foragers.
    True or False

23. Today we know that, especially in the humid tropics, slash-and-burn agriculture may be one of the best gardening techniques possible.
True or False

24. It can be safely said that "preindustrial" cities are very uncommon in today's world.
True or False

25. All innovations turn out to be positive in the long run, eventually improving conditions for every member of a society.
True or False

26. Everybody benefits from changes, even if they are forced upon them.
True or False

27. Notwithstanding the multiple changes that have occurred over the course of many thousands of years, the original division of labor has been eliminated from every culture.
True or False

28. Today industrialism is declining rapidly.
True or False

Practice Matching

1. _____ Tsembaga
2. _____ Bakhtiari
3. _____ Comanche
4. _____ Mbuti
5. _____ Montagnais

a. They live in Labrador.
b. West Asian pastoralists.
c. Horse people of the Great Plains.
d. Pig sacrificers of New Guinea.
e. Food foragers of the Ituri rain forest.

Practice Short Answer Questions

1. Explain why the development of farming in Southwest Asia and Mesoamerica was considered a case of parallel evolution.

2. Explain why anthropologist Marshall Sahlins referred to food foragers as the "original affluent society."

3. What are the characteristics of an agricultural society?

4. Why do anthropologists not use the term "progress"?

5. Distinguish between food-foraging societies and food-producing societies.

Practice Essays

1. How does Ju/'hoansi social organization relate to the subsistence pattern of hunting and collecting? How is Ju/'hoansi society likely to change as the foraging way of life erodes?

2. Think about your neighborhood. Could it be described as a kind of cultural area, i.e., a geographic region in which a number of different societies follow similar patterns of life? What criteria would be important for defining it that way?

3. The Mekranoti Kayapo employ what has come to be known as slash-and-burn agriculture. Describe the benefits of this style of farming in the tropics. What would be the consequences of a U.S.-style of agriculture in the tropics?

4. As mentioned in your textbook, just as we have much to learn from the successes of indigenous peoples, so can we learn from their mistakes, and the ways they cope with their mistakes. Anthropologist Ann Kendall is doing just this in southern Peru. What did her research discover and what is she doing to rectify the results of the past mistakes of indigenous peoples in the Patacacha Valley in the Andes Mountains?

5. Explain how the anthropologist was able to calculate the productivity of Mekranoti gardens.

6. It is said that "environments do not determine culture but do set certain potentials and limitations." Provide examples to support this statement.

7. What impact has intensive agriculture had on human society?

8. Discuss how the Great Plains became an indigenous culture area.

9. Describe the negative stereotype of food foragers. How did it come about and why is it ill-founded?

Solutions

Fill-in-the-Blank

1. Adaptation
2. ecosystem
3. buffalo
4. convergent
5. parallel
6. area
7. food foraging
8. density of social relations
9. transhumance
10. Ethnoscientists
11. 10,000
12. agriculture
13. carrying capacity
14. 60–70
15. meat
16. swidden
17. Pastoral nomads
18. agriculture
19. Tenochtitlan
20. Ann Kendall

Multiple-Choice Practice Questions

1. A
2. E
3. C
4. E
5. B
6. D
7. C
8. E
9. C
10. A
11. B
12. D
13. B
14. B
15. D
16. E
17. B
18. D
19. E
20. E
21. E
22. B
23. A
24. E
25. E
26. C
27. C
28. C
29. E
30. E
31. B
32. E
33. C
34. D
35. B

True/False Practice Questions

1. F
2. T
3. T
4. T
5. T
6. F
7. T
8. F
9. T
10. F
11. F
12. F
13. T
14. F
15. F
16. F
17. F
18. T
19. F
20. F
21. T
22. F
23. T
24. F
25. F
26. F
27. F
28. F

Practice Matching

1. D
2. B
3. C
4. E
5. A

Chapter 8

Economic Systems

Synopsis

Challenge Issues: How do anthropologists study economic systems? How do different societies organize their economic resources and labor? How and why are goods exchanged or redistributed? This chapter discusses the attempt to apply economic theory to non-Western cultures and summarizes the concepts anthropologists have developed to compare the organization of productive resources across cultures. The authors describe the major ways of distributing goods and services through reciprocity, redistribution, and market exchange. This chapter also considers the relevance of anthropological understanding applied to this era of globalization.

Chapter Objectives

I. economic anthropology

II. production and its resources

III. distribution and exchange

IV. local cultures and economic globalization

Key Terms

balanced reciprocity
conspicuous consumption
economic system
generalized reciprocity
informal economy
Kula ring
leveling mechanism
market exchange

money
negative reciprocity
potlatch
prestige economy
reciprocity
redistribution
silent trade
technology

Exercises

The Anthropology Resource Center (ARC)

The Anthropology Resource Center is a dynamic, subfield-specific website that provides a wealth of materials for both students and instructors to reinforce key concepts in anthropology. All of the resources and activities encourage students to apply anthropology beyond the textbook and classroom. ARC can be reached through the weblink http://thomsonedu.com/. After selecting the discipline of "Anthropology" under "Humanities and Social Sciences," go directly to ARC for a wide range of resources that bring anthropology to life through pictures, interviews, news items, interactive displays, maps, and more. (This site is passcode-protected for both instructors and students.)

Review Questions

1. Why might it be misleading to apply contemporary economic theories to preindustrial non-Western societies?

2. Explain the importance of yam production among the Trobrianders.

3. Provide examples that refute the notion of a division of labor by gender.

4. Compare and contrast the three general patterns of the division of labor by gender.

5. What are the benefits of the division of labor by age?

6. How is land controlled in most preindustrial societies?

7. Differentiate between the use of tools in foraging, horticultural, and agricultural communities.

8. Distinguish between industrial and nonindustrial societies with regard to craft specialization.

9. How do societies cooperate in the acquisition of food?

10. Provide some examples of leveling mechanisms.

11. Distinguish between market exchange and marketplace.

12. What are three systems of exchange?

13. What purpose does reciprocity serve?

14. Differentiate between general, balanced, and negative reciprocity.

15. How is trade between groups generally conducted?

16. What were the primary contributions of Jomo Kenyatta?

17. What functions does the Kula ring serve?

18. What is money?

19. Describe redistribution among the Inca.

20. Describe the "informal economy" of North America.

21. How is conspicuous consumption used?

22. Discuss the relevance of anthropology to international business.

23. What are the drawbacks of ethnocentric interpretations of other societies' economic systems?

24. Discuss the role that culture plays in defining the "wants and needs" of a people.

Fill-in-the-Blank

1. All societies have rules pertaining to three productive resources: _____, _____, and _____.

2. Division of labor by gender varies from very flexible to very rigid. Among foragers like the _____, either sex may do the work of the other without loss of face.

3. When two or more partners from different groups negotiate a direct exchange of one trade good for another, it is called _____.

4. In most societies the basic unit in which cooperation takes place is the _____.

5. Among horticulturalists, tools that are typically used are the _____, _____, and _____.

6. A _____ spreads wealth around so that no one accumulates substantially more wealth than anyone else.

7. _____ was the first to carry out a scientific investigation of the Kula ring.

8. Types of reciprocity are _____, _____, and _____.

9. The taxation systems of Canada and the United States are examples of _____.

10. In some societies the surplus is used as a display for purposes of prestige. This is called _____.

11. Money is believed to have first been used about _____ in Mesopotamia.

12. A(n) _____ is a network of producing and circulating marketable commodities, labor, and services that escape government control.

Multiple-Choice Practice Questions

1. When a man works hard in his horticultural garden in the Trobriand Islands to produce yams, he does this to satisfy which of the following demands?
   a. to have food for his household to eat
   b. to gain prestige by giving yams away to his sisters' husbands
   c. to prove to his wife that he can work as hard as she can
   d. to give the yams to his wife so that she can trade them for goods that they don't produce themselves
   e. to trade for fish

2. The productive resources used by all societies to produce goods and services include _____.
   a. raw materials
   b. labor
   c. technology
   d. bureaucrats
   e. raw materials, labor and technology

3. American society's traditional sexual division of labor falls into which pattern?
   a. flexible
   b. rigid segregation
   c. segregation with equality
   d. integrated
   e. cooperative

4. Among the Ju/'hoansi _____.
   a. children are expected to contribute to subsistence from the time they are seven or eight.
   b. elderly people past the age of sixty are expected to contribute hunted or gathered food to the group.
   c. elderly people are a valuable source of knowledge and wisdom about hunting and gathering.
   d. elderly people are taken care of grudgingly because after the age of sixty they contribute nothing to the group.
   e. children are expected to set up their own separate households by the time they are twelve.

5. In many nonindustrial societies, _____.
   a. people prefer to have fun rather than to work
   b. cooperative work is usually done with a festive, sociable air
   c. cooperative work is always done in the household
   d. cooperative work groups are organized primarily for profit
   e. solitary work is preferred to cooperative work

6. Among food foragers such as the Ju/'hoansi, _____.
   a. land is defined as a territory with usable resources and flexible boundaries that belongs to a band that has occupied it for a long time
   b. land is thought of as belonging to those who have bought it
   c. land is considered private property, and access to the land can be denied
   d. land has clear-cut boundaries marked by survey posts
   e. land is controlled by a corporation of strangers

7. In nonindustrial societies, when a tool is complex and difficult to make it is usually considered to be owned by _____.
   a. the whole village in which it is used
   b. a single individual
   c. the state
   d. all those who touch it
   e. all relatives

8. Leveling mechanisms _____.
   a. are more common in hunter-gatherer societies than in agricultural communities
   b. result in one family becoming wealthier than others
   c. are found in communities where property must not be allowed to threaten an egalitarian social order
   d. are more common in industrial societies than in agricultural societies
   e. no longer exist

9. The mode of distribution called reciprocity refers to the exchange of goods and services _____.
   a. of unequal value
   b. between persons in hierarchical relationships
   c. for the purpose of maintaining social relationships and gaining prestige
   d. to make a profit
   e. to embarrass the person who gave the least

10. A Navaho gives ten of his sheep that he knows are infected with disease to a Hopi in exchange for a jeep. This is an example of _____.
    a. generalized reciprocity
    b. balanced reciprocity
    c. negative reciprocity
    d. silent trade
    e. redistribution

11. The Kula ring _____.
    a. is a marriage ring made of shells
    b. is found among the Ju/'hoansi
    c. is found among the Andaman Islanders
    d. is a circular trade route along which various goods flow
    e. is a form of silent trade

12. The American system of paying income taxes every April is an example of _____.
    a. generalized reciprocity
    b. balanced reciprocity
    c. negative reciprocity
    d. redistribution
    e. market exchange

13. The display of wealth for social prestige is called _____.
    a. a leveling mechanism
    b. conspicuous consumption
    c. redistribution
    d. balanced reciprocity
    e. barter

14. Formal market exchange is usually associated with _____.
    a. hunting and gathering bands
    b. horticultural tribes
    c. pastoral tribes
    d. a state type of political organization
    e. the household as the unit of production and consumption

15. A businessperson who wants to build a factory in the Middle East could benefit from the contributions of a cultural anthropologist. In which of the following ways would an anthropologist be likely to help?
    a. provide knowledge of the principles of market exchange
    b. introduce a new method of paying local workers
    c. tell the businessperson how to sit, dress, and talk when making the arrangements with local people
    d. screen workers who have diseases
    e. "introduce a new method of paying local workers", "tell the businessperson how to sit, dress, and talk when making the arrangements with local people"

16. Silent trade is a specialized form of _____.
    a. informal economy
    b. barter
    c. prestige economy
    d. conspicuous consumption
    e. money

17. Which of the following was **not** an exchange partner with the others?
    a. Badaga
    b. Kurumba
    c. Inca
    d. Toda
    e. Kota

18. Not only have anthropologists found niches for themselves in the world of business, but since 1972, the number of them going into business has grown _____.
    a. tenfold
    b. fivefold
    c. 50 percent
    d. 1000 percent
    e. 25 percent

19. One of the newest innovations in the market-research and design industry is _____.
    a. survey questionnaire
    b. telephone surveys
    c. ethnology
    d. ethnography
    e. case studies

20. The Inca Empire was known for practicing _____.
    a. generalized reciprocity
    b. balanced reciprocity

   c. negative reciprocity

   d. redistribution

   e. conspicuous consumption

21. One successful anthropologist working in corporate America doing international consulting for a large computer firm is _____.

   a. Vicki Cassman

   b. Jennifer Thompson

   c. Karen Stephenson

   d. Laura Nader

   e. Jomo Kenyatta

22. Which of the following was a form of money for the Aztecs?

   a. feathers

   b. salt

   c. yams

   d. cacao

   e. coconuts

23. An anthropologist interested in the systems of production, exchange, and redistribution would be called a(n) _____ anthropologist.

   a. political

   b. linguistic

   c. economic

   d. physical

   e. psychological

24. The division of labor by gender that has been described as the flexible/integrated pattern is found among which of the following?

   a. Bakhtiari

   b. Ju/'hoansi

   c. Taiwanese

   d. Dahomeans

   e. industrial countries

25. One example of specialization is afforded by the _____ people of Ethiopia's Danakil Depression. The men of this group are miners of salt.

   a. Nuer

   b. Azande

   c. Hadza

   d. Afar

   c. Ashanti

26. A societal obligation compelling a family to distribute goods so that no one accumulates more wealth than anyone else is referred to by anthropologists as a _____.

    a. flat tax

    b. commune

    c. capital gains tax

    d. poverty spreader

    e. leveling mechanism

27. In economic anthropology, a mode of exchange in which the value of the gift is not calculated, nor is the time of repayment specified is known as _____.

    a. charity

    b. generosity

    c. a handout

    d. generalized reciprocity

    e. Christmas

28. In political fund-raising in the United States large contributors expect that their "generosity" will buy influence with a candidate. What category of reciprocity would this fall under?

    a. derisive

    b. negative

    c. general

    d. balanced

    e. none of these

29. Not all trade is motivated by economic considerations. A classic case of this is _____.

    a. silent trade

    b. the swap meet

    c. the flea market

    d. the Kula ring

    e. the *cargo* system

30. Among the _____, both cacao beans and cotton cloaks served as money.

    a. Tiv

    b. Aztecs

    c. Enga

    d. Trobriand Islanders

    e. Inca

31. The Kula ring is a form of _____ that reinforces trade relations among a group of seafaring Melanesians inhabiting a ring of islands off the eastern coast of Papua New Guinea.

    a. negative reciprocity

    b. balanced reciprocity

    c. market exchange

d. silent trade

e. generalized reciprocity

32. _____ first described the Kula ring, he observed it during ethnographic research among the Trobriand Islanders between 1915-1918.

a. Franz Boas

b. Gordon Childe

c. Bronislaw Malinowski

d. Margaret Mead

e. A. R. Radcliffe-Brown

33. Harvard-trained anthropologist _____ uses anthropological tools to research and analyze corporate "cultures" in order to help them solve problems and improve performance.

a. Karen Stephenson

b. Karen Harry

c. Barbara Roth

d. Jennifer Thompson

e. Steve Barnett

True/False Practice Questions

1. The Trobriands are in South America.
   True or False

2. In "silent trade," no words are spoken, but the participants must meet face to face to exchange goods.
   True or False

3. The Inca empire of Peru featured a highly efficient redistributive system.
   True or False

4. The number and kind of tools a society uses are related to its lifestyle.
   True or False

5. In the integrated pattern of labor, men and women carry out their work separately.
   True or False

6. Jomo Kenyatta was an anthropologist who became "the father" of modern Kenya.
   True or False

7. In societies without a money economy, the rewards of labor are never direct.
   True or False

8. There are three modes of redistribution.
   True or False

9. Anthropologists only work in exotic, faraway places like remote islands, deep forests, hostile deserts, or arctic wastelands.
   True or False

10. There is a potential job market for anthropologists in the market-research and design area.
    True or False

11. According to your textbook, most anthropologists who work at market-research and design companies are not really "doing ethnography."
    True or False

12. Doing research in corporate America is not so different from doing initial anthropological research in an unfamiliar culture.
    True or False

13. Trobriand Island men devote a great deal of time and energy to raise yams, not for themselves but to give to others.
    True or False

14. No specialization of labor craft exists in nonindustrial societies.
    True or False

15. Anthropologists have found no form of conspicuous consumption occurring in nonindustrial societies.
    True or False

16. In non-Western societies the market is an important focus of social as well as economic activity.
    True or False

17. In Africa, much of the farming is the job of women. Failure to accept this fact is responsible for the failure of many development schemes, since outside experts design projects that usually assume the men in society are the farmers.
    True or False

18. The Kula ring used to involve thousands of men but no longer functions today.
    True or False

19. Anthropological research methods work well when conducting cross-cultural research, but are worthless in studying the modern corporate way of life.
    True or False

20. Corporations headquartered in the so-called developed world are in business not only to make a profit, but to protect the weak, benefit the poor, support the sick, and save the environment.
    True or False

Practice Short Answer Questions

1. Describe and discuss the new form of market exchange that has developed in industrial and post-industrial societies.

2. What is meant by the term "savage capitalism?"

3. Describe and provide examples of each of the three forms of reciprocity.

4. How does the Inca Empire exhibit redistribution?

5. Compare and contrast leveling mechanism and prestige economy.

6. What is an informal economy?

7. Describe the economic system of the Ju/'hoansi.

Practice Essays

1. Compare and contrast the different ideas about the nature and control of land that exist among food foragers, horticulturalists, pastoralists, intensive agriculturalists, and industrialists.

2. Compare and contrast the different ideas about tools and tool ownership in foraging, horticultural, and intensive agricultural societies.

3. Describe what an anthropologist can contribute to the world of business.

4. Compare and contrast a prestige economy with an economy based on conspicuous consumption.

5. Specify and elaborate on the three categories of distribution of material goods.

6. What is money? What impact did its introduction have on culture?

9. Because trade can be essential in the quest for survival and is often undertaken for the sake of luxury, people may go to great lengths to establish and maintain good trade relations. A classic example of this is the Kula ring. What is the Kula ring? Describe.

10. Discuss Karen Stephenson's work in corporate anthropology. How is her work different from the work of more traditional anthropologists?

Solutions

Fill-in-the-Blank

1. production, exchange, redistribution
2. Ju /'hoansi
3. barter
4. household
5. axe, digging stick, hoe
6. leveling mechanism
7. Bronislaw Malinowski
8. reciprocity, redistribution, exchange
9. redistribution
10. conspicuous consumption
11. 5,000
12. informal economy

Multiple-Choice Practice Questions

1. B
2. E
3. B
4. C
5. B
6. A
7. B
8. C
9. C
10. C
11. D
12. D
13. B
14. D
15. E
16. B
17. C
18. B
19. D
20. D
21. C
22. D
23. C
24. B
25. D
26. E
27. D
28. D
29. D
30. B
31. B
32. C
33. A

True/False Practice Questions

1. F
2. F
3. T
4. T
5. F
6. T
7. F
8. F
9. F
10. T
11. T
12. T
13. T
14. F
15. F
16. T
17. T
18. F
19. F
20. F

Chapter 9

Sex and Marriage

Synopsis

Challenge Issues: What is marriage? What is the family? What is the difference between family and household? This chapter defines marriage as a system for regulating sexual access and explores varieties of marriage throughout the world. The authors consider how marriage is adaptive, focusing on ways that family and household compositions vary in response to particular social, historical, and ecological circumstances.

Chapter Objectives

I.   control of sexual relations

II. forms of marriage

III. choice of spouse

IV. marriage and economic exchange

V.   divorce

VI. family and household

VII. marriage, family, and household in our globalized and technologized world

Key Terms

affinal kin
ambilocal residence
bride-price
bride service
conjugal family
consanguineal family
consanguineal kin
cross cousin
dowry
endogamy
exogamy
extended family
family
fictive marriage

group marriage
household
incest taboo
marriage
matrilocal residence
monogamy
neolocal residence
nuclear family
parallel cousin
patrilocal residence
polyandry
polygamy
polygyny
serial monogamy

Exercises

The Anthropology Resource Center (ARC)

The Anthropology Resource Center is a dynamic, subfield-specific website that provides a wealth of materials for both students and instructors to reinforce key concepts in anthropology. All of the resources and activities encourage students to apply anthropology beyond the textbook and classroom. ARC can be reached through the weblink http://thomsonedu.com/. After selecting the discipline of "Anthropology" under "Humanities and Social Sciences," go directly to ARC for a wide range of resources that bring anthropology to life through pictures, interviews, news items, interactive displays, maps, and more. (This site is passcode-protected for both instructors and students.)

Review Questions

1. Why are human females able to engage in sexual activity regardless of their ovulation cycles?

2. Why does sexual activity require social control?

3. Describe the sex life of the Trobrianders.

4. As discussed in your textbook, describe the traditional marriage system of the Nayar.

5. What is the incest taboo?

6. Why do people who live in close proximity to one another exhibit reduced sexual activity?

7. What is the difference between a family and a household?

8. How have geneticists and anthropologists attempted to explain the incest taboo?

9. Distinguish between endogamy and exogamy.

10. What were the initial reasons for exogamy, according to Levi-Strauss?

11. Distinguish between marriage and mating.

12. To what extent can North American society be characterized as monogamous?

13. Provide a non-ethnocentric definition of marriage.

14. Distinguish between consanguineal and conjugal families.

15. Distinguish between polygynous and polyandrous families.

16. What form of marriage does the majority of the world's societies exhibit?

17. Characterize the typical polygynous society.

18. What are the various residence patterns found cross culturally?

19. Describe the social and economic context of polyandry.

20. Discuss the contexts in which sororate, levirate, and serial monogamy are likely to occur.

21. What benefits do arranged marriages have?

22. What is the role of new reproductive technologies on the composition of families today?

23. Distinguish between patrilateral parallel-cousin and matrilateral cross-cousin marriage.

24. What is fictive marriage?

25. Distinguish between bride price, dowry, and bride service.

26. What is the function of female-female marriage among the Nandi?

27. What role can anthropologists play in the study of AIDS?

Fill-in-the-Blank

1. Marriage is a cultural transaction that regulates men's and women's rights of _____ access to one another and defines the context in which women are eligible to bear children.

2. _____ residence is where the newly-married couple form a new residence apart from family.

3. Only about _____ percent of the world's societies prohibit all sexual involvement outside of marriage.

4. The bond between two individuals joined by marriage is called a(n) _____ bond.

5. Households composed only of "blood" relatives are said to contain _____ kin.

6. The _____ taboo prohibits sexual relations between specified individuals.

7. _____ is a rule mandating the one marry outside of a particular group, while _____ mandates marriage within the group.

8. In the United States, _____ is the only legally recognized form of marriage, but some Americans do engage in other forms.

9. A _____ family contains a husband and his multiple wives, while a family contains a wife and her multiple husbands.

10. _____ is the preferred form of marriage worldwide

11. When the wives in a polygynous marriage are sisters, this is called _____ polygyny.

12. _____ marriage refers to a marriage in which several men and women have sexual access to one another.

13. In a _____, a widow marries the brother of her deceased husband; in a , a widower marries the sister of his deceased wife.

14. Marrying a sequence of partners throughout one's life is called _____.

15. In a patrilateral parallel-cousin marriage, a boy marries his father's _____ daughter.

16. _____ is a gift exchange occurring at marriage in which money or goods are transferred from the groom's side to the bride's.

17. In a _____ system, the bride's family provides money or goods at the time of marriage.

18. The Nandi of western Kenya practice a form of marriage in which a woman marries _____.

19. Divorce rates in Western society are at approximately _____ percent.

20. _____ is a French anthropologist who launched a school of thought called structuralism.

21. _____ marriage is marriage by proxy.

Multiple-Choice Practice Questions

1. _____ is a transaction in which a woman and man establish a continuing claim to the right of sexual access to one another, and in which the woman involved becomes eligible to bear children.
   a. Family
   b. Marriage
   c. Incest
   d. Affinity
   e. Sex

2. _____ residence is when the newly-married couple may choose to live with the wife's mother's or husband's father's family.
   a. ambilocal
   b. avunculocal
   c. patrilocal
   d. matrilocal
   e. neolocal

3. Marriage resolves the problem of how to bring sexual activity under _____ control.
   a. biological
   b. male
   c. cultural
   d. female
   e. mother-in-law

4. A household composed of married people contains _____ kin.
   a. affinal
   b. consanguineal
   c. endogamous
   d. nuclear
   e. instinctive

5. Two or more closely related nuclear families clustered together in a large domestic group is a(n) _____ family.
   a. nuclear
   b. nontraditional
   c. extended
   d. blended
   e. conjugal

6. Although all societies have some kind of incest taboo, the relationship that is considered incestuous may vary. Concepts of incest seem to be related to a group's definitions of endogamy and exogamy, thus suggesting that incest taboos may help to promote _____.

    a. alliances between groups

    b. inbreeding

    c. brother-sister marriages

    d. parallel-cousin marriages

    e. cross-cousin marriages

7. Marriage within a particular group of individuals is called _____.

    a. incest

    b. exogamy

    c. monogamy

    d. endogamy

    e. polygamy

8. The French anthropologist Claude Levi-Strauss says that the incest taboo is universal because humans _____.

    a. are instinctively opposed to inbreeding

    b. repress their sexual desire for the parent of the opposite sex

    c. have learned to establish alliances with strangers and thereby share and develop culture

    d. prefer to marry their brothers and sisters

    e. do not like sex

9. A residential kin group composed of a woman, her dependent children, and at least one adult male joined through marriage or blood relationship is a/an _____.

    a. family

    b. conjugal bond

    c. endogamous

    d. nuclear family

    e. serial marriage

10. Families can be consanguineal or conjugal. The conjugal family has many forms. One type of conjugal family is the _____, consisting of the husband, wife, and dependent children.

    a. polygynous family

    b. polygamous family

    c. polyandrous family

    d. nuclear family

    e. extended family

11. Although _____ may statistically be the most common form of marriage around the world, it is not the most preferred.

    a. polygyny

    b. monogamy

    c. polyandry

    d. polygamy

    e. the levirate

12. Polygyny _____.

    a. means marriage to more than one man

    b. is the most common form of marriage

    c. is usually possible only when a man is fairly wealthy

    d. is less common than polyandry

    e. is an example of group marriage

13. An example of group marriage would be _____.

    a. a pastoral nomad's wife among the Turkana who actively searches for another woman to share her husband and her work with the livestock.

    b. the Moonies having a large wedding ceremony at which five hundred couples, each one assigned to another, are married at the same time.

    c. a prosperous member of the Kapauku in western New Guinea who is able to afford a bride price for four wives.

    d. a hippy commune in the Haight-Ashbury district in which it is accepted that all adult members of the commune have sexual access to each other.

    e. a Nayar household in which a woman takes several lovers.

14. The levirate and the sororate _____.

    a. are secret societies, like sororities and fraternities.

    b. function to maintain the relationship between the family of the bride and the family of the groom.

    c. are usually possible only when the man is fairly wealthy

    d. are types of cattle in pastoralist societies

    e. exist only in advanced industrial societies

15. Serial monogamy tends to occur in societies where _____.

    a. a woman with children receives a great deal of help from her mother and brothers

    b. women do not have many children

    c. a woman with dependent children, isolated from her parents, marries a series of partners to get the assistance of another adult

    d. women are very wealthy

    e. divorce is forbidden

16. The main function of a bride price is _____.

    a. for a man to show off to his wife how rich he is

    b. for a man to buy a slave

    c. for the wife's people to gain prestige in the village

    d. to compensate the wife's family for her labor

    e. for the wife's people to buy a husband for their daughter

17. When a man marries his father's brother's daughter in ancient Greece or traditional China, _____.

    a. he is committing incest

    b. he is practicing matrilineal cross-cousin marriage

    c. he is practicing patrilateral parallel-cousin marriage

    d. he is keeping property within the single male line of descent

    e. "he is practicing patrilateral parallel-cousin marriage", "he is keeping property within the single male line of descent"

18. In which of the following situations would you expect to find the custom of bride price?

    a. a bride and groom leave the community after marriage and set up their own household in a distant city

    b. a bride and groom go to live with the bride's people

    c. a bride and groom go to live with the groom's people

    d. a bride and groom go to live with the bride's mother's brother

    e. none of these

19. When the economy is based on _____ and where the man does most of the productive work, the bride's people may give a dowry that protects the woman against desertion and is a statement of her economic status.

    a. food foraging

    b. pastoralism

    c. intensive agriculture

    d. horticulture

    e. industrialism

20. The woman/woman marriage custom found in sub-Saharan Africa _____.

    a. enables a woman without sons to inherit a share of her husband's property

    b. confers legitimacy on the children of a woman who had been unable to find a husband

    c. enables the woman who adopts a male identity to raise her status

    d. enables the woman who is the wife of the female husband to raise her status and live a more secure life

    e. "enables a woman without sons to inherit a share of her husband's property", "confers legitimacy on the children of a woman who had been unable to find a husband.", "enables the woman who adopts a male identity to raise her status" and "enables the woman who is the wife of the female husband to raise her status and live a more secure life"

21. Which of the following constitutes a culturally valid reason for divorce among different groups?

    a. sterility or impotence

    b. cruelty

    c. being a poor provider

    d. being a lazy housekeeper

    e. "sterility or impotence", "cruelty", "being a poor provider" and "being a lazy housekeeper"

22. A residence pattern in which a married couple lives in the wife's mother's place of residence is _____ residence.

    a. avunculocal

    b. ambilocal

    c. neolocal

    d. matrilocal

    e. patrilocal

23. According to the article in your textbook "Arranging Marriage in India," among urban Indians an important source of contacts in trying to arrange a marriage is/are the _____.

    a. social club

    b. newspaper personals

    c. internet chat rooms

    d. match making businesses

    e. temple

24. Which of the following characteristics would be most important in an Indian family's selection of a bride for their son?

    a. good looks

    b. well-educated

    c. independent

    d. have higher social status

    e. good character

25. _____ is the leading exponent of French structuralism.

    a. Bronislaw Malinowski

    b. Franz Boas

    c. Claude Levi-Strauss

    d. Phillipe Cousteau

    e. Emile Durkheim

26. What sets _____ apart is that sex may occur even when the female is not swollen.

    a. chimpanzees

    b. bonobos

    c. macaques

    d. orangutangs

    e. gorillas

27. According to your text, in the United States there are somewhere between 20,000 and
 _____ people in the Rocky Mountain states that live in households made up of a man with
 two or more wives.

    a. 100,000

    b. 75,000

    c. 15,000

    d. 1 million

    e. 60,000

28. A(n) _____ family is established through marriage.

    a. nuclear

    b. extended

    c. affinal

    d. consanguineal

    e. conjugal

29. No societies have achieved greater separation between the sexual and reproductive attributes
 of women than the _____.

    a. Nandi

    b. Nayar

    c. Azande

    d. Mundugamor

    e. United States and other Western countries

30. _____ marriage is when several men and women have sexual access to one another.

    a. fictive

    b. group

    c. affinal

    d. conjugal

    e. nontraditional

31. In the United States, as in most Western countries, _____ is the only legally recognized
 form of marriage.

    a. polygamy

    b. polygyny

    c. monogamy

    d. polyandry

    e. serial

32. Most divorced people in the United States remarry at least once. Thus, _____ is not
 uncommon.

    a. polygamy

    b. serial monogamy

c. sororate marriage

d. levirate marriage

e. polyandry

33. Conjugal families are formed on the basis of marital ties between husband and wife. Which of the following are forms of conjugal families?

   a. polyandrous families

   b. consanguine families

   c. polygynous families

   d. nuclear families

   e. polyandrous families, polygynous families and nuclear families

34. In some societies when a woman marries she receives her share of the family inheritance, or her _____.

   a. bride price

   b. bride service

   c. dowry

   d. bride commission

   e. birthright

35. Among the _____ of Kenya, sterility or impotence were grounds for divorce.

   a. Eritreans

   b. Gusii

   c. Nandi

   d. Hutu

   e. Chenchu

36. In some societies, preferred marriages are a man marrying his father's brother's daughter. This is known as patrilateral parallel-cousin marriage. Although not obligatory, such marriages have been favored historically among which of the following cultures?

   a. traditional Chinese

   b. Arabs

   c. ancient Greece

   d. ancient Israelites

   e. traditional Chinese, Arabs, ancient Greece and ancient Israelites

37. Only a minority of known societies, about _____ percent, have rules requiring that sexual involvement take place only within marriage.

   a. 25

   b. 15

   c. 10

   d. 5

   e. 30

38. In which of the following countries is same-sex marriages considered socially acceptable and allowed by law?
    a. Mexico
    b. Canada
    c. Italy
    d. the Netherlands
    e. B and D

39. A culturally sanctioned union between two or more persons that established certain rights and obligations between the persons, between them and their children, and between them and their in-laws.
    a. monogamy
    b. conjugal bond
    c. endogamy
    d. exogamy
    e. marriage

True/False Practice Questions

1. Trobriand children begin sexual experimentation at a young age.
   True or False

2. About half of the world's societies prohibit sexual involvement outside of marriage.
   True or False

3. There is only one type of family.
   True or False

4. Brother-sister marriages were common among farmers in Roman Egypt.
   True or False

5. Matrilocal residence is when the couple goes to live with the husband's mother's family.
   True or False

6. People want pretty much the same things in marriage whether it is in India or America.
   True or False

7. Today, a dowry is expected by law in India.
   True or False

8. In India it is understood that matches (marriages) would be arranged only within the same caste and general social class.
   True or False

9. In India no crossing of subcastes is permissible even if the class positions of the bride's and groom's families are similar.
   True or False

10. As far as arranging a marriage is concerned, in India the basic rule seems to be that a family's reputation is most important.
    True or False

11. Fictive marriage is also called marriage by proxy.
    True or False

12. Neolocal residence is when the newly married couple establishes their own new household apart from their families.
    True or False

13. Extended families are rare.
    True or False

14. Group marriage is also called co-marriage.
    True or False

15. There is such a thing as double-proxy marriage.
    True or False

16. A household is the same thing as a family.
    True or False

17. First-cousin marriage is no longer considered to be genetically risky.
    True or False

18. Bonobos will not engage in sex when a female is pregnant.
    True or False

19. Both cross-cultural studies, and those of other animals, suggest that homosexual behavior is unnatural.
    True or False

20. In a number of societies researchers have discovered that same-sex marriages are regarded as perfectly appropriate.
    True or False

21. A parallel cousin is the child of a father's brother.
    True or False

22. In the United States today, single-parent households outnumber nuclear family households.
    True or False

23. A cross cousin is the child of a mother's brother.
    True or False

24. Divorce is possible in all societies, though reasons for divorce as well as its frequency vary widely from one society to another.
    True or False

25. There are no cultures that prescribe male-to-male sexual acts, for any reason.
    True or False

26. The social rules and cultural meanings of all sexual behavior are subject to great variability from one society to another.
    True or False

27. Marriage, as pointed out in your textbook, always involves the establishment of a new family.
    True or False

Practice Matching

Match the culture with its characteristic.

1. _____ Nandi

2. _____ Aborigines of Australia

3. _____ Nayar

4. _____ Tibetans

5. _____ North Americans

a. A culture emphasizing love and choice as a basis for marriage.

b. South Indian people who give the mother's brothers key responsibility in child rearing.

c. a group that favors matrilateral cross-cousin marriage

d. East African pastoralists who practice woman/woman marriage.

e. Polyandrous society of central Asia.

Short Answer Practice Questions

1. What is the positive outcome of having strict religious rules that regulate sexual relations?

2. Explain why your textbook's definition of marriage refers to "persons" rather than "a man and a woman."

3. Describe the various forms of residence pattern.

4. Distinguish between parallel and cross cousins.

5. What is the difference between marriage and mating?

6. What are some effects of new reproductive technologies on the composition of family today?

7. What is the effect of globalization on the family today?

8. Explain the incest taboo.

Practice Essays

1. Discuss how various societies have sought to regulate sexual relations.

2. Explain the universality of the incest taboo and describe its cross-cultural variation.

3. Describe how the "romantic love" complex impacts North American marriage patterns. Is romantic love involved in marriage in India? Discuss why or why not?

4. What factors affect the stability of marriages and the choice of mates?

5. What factors must be taken into consideration when arranging a marriage in India? Describe.

6. Describe the Nayar and their rules of sexual access.

7. Anthropologists have found that universally societies have cultural rules that act to control sexual relations. What are the rules of sexual access from one culture to another?

8. What is the "incest taboo?" Explain why it is such a challenge for anthropologists to explain in terms of its universality and why incest commonly should be regarded as such loathsome behavior?

9. Explain the distinction between marriage and mating.

10. Discuss the arrangement of marriage in India.

11. Expound on the reasons and frequency of divorce from society to society.

Solutions

Fill-in-the-Blank

1. sexual
2. Neolocal
3. five
4. conjugal
5. consanguineal
6. incest
7. Exogamy, endogamy
8. monogamy
9. polygynous, polyandrous
10. polygamy
11. sororal
12. Group
13. levirate, sororate
14. serial marriage
15. brother's
16. Bride price
17. dowry
18. woman
19. matrilineal
20. Claude Levi-Strauss
21. Fictive

Multiple-Choice Practice Questions

1. B
2. A
3. C
4. A
5. C
6. A
7. D
8. C
9. A
10. D
11. B
12. C
13. D
14. B
15. C
16. D
17. E
18. C
19. C
20. E
21. E
22. D
23. A
24. E
25. C
26. B
27. E
28. E
29. E
30. B
31. C
32. B
33. E
34. C
35. B
36. E
37. B
38. E
39. E

True/False Practice Questions

1. T
2. F
3. F
4. T
5. F
6. F
7. F
8. T
9. F
10. T
11. T
12. T
13. F
14. T
15. T
16. F
17. T
18. F
19. F
20. T
21. T
22. T
23. T
24. T
25. F
26. T
27. F

Practice Matching

1. D
2. C
3. B
4. E
5. A

Chapter 10

Kinship and Descent

Synopsis

Challenge Issues: What is kinship? What are descent groups? What functions do kin-ordered groups serve? This chapter presents key concepts relating to the anthropological study of kinship and descent, including the varieties of descent group and the organization and function of these groups as adaptive mechanisms. The chapter also includes the primary systems of kinship terminology and the challenges that technology presents to the traditional notions of kinship.

Chapter Objectives

    I.   descent groups

   II.   descent integrated into the cultural system

  III.   bilateral kinship and the kindred

  IV.   cultural evolution of the descent group

   V.   kinship terminology and descent groups

Key Terms

clan
descent group
EGO
Eskimo system
Fission
Hawaiian system
Iroquois system
kindred
kinship

lineage
matrilineal descent
moiety
new reproductive technologies
patrilineal descent
phratry
totemism
unilineal descent

Exercises

The Anthropology Resource Center (ARC)

The Anthropology Resource Center is a dynamic, subfield-specific website that provides a wealth of materials for both students and instructors to reinforce key concepts in anthropology. All of the resources and activities encourage students to apply anthropology beyond the textbook and classroom. ARC can be reached through the weblink http://thomsonedu.com/. After selecting the discipline of "Anthropology" under "Humanities and Social Sciences," go directly to ARC for a wide range of resources that bring anthropology to life through pictures, interviews, news items, interactive displays, maps, and more. (This site is passcode-protected for both instructors and students.)

Review Questions

1. Why do societies form descent groups?

2. How is membership in a descent group restricted?

3. Distinguish between patrilineal and matrilineal descent groups

4. What function does double descent serve?

5. Explain the function of ambilineal descent in contemporary North America. Provide an example.

6. What functions do descent groups serve?

7. How is a lineage reckoned?

8. What are the social implications of lineage exogamy?

9. Contrast a clan and a lineage.

10. What did anthropologist Harald Prins do for the Micmac Indians?

11. What purpose do totems serve a clan?

12. Distinguish between a phratry and a moiety.

13. How do bilateral systems differ from unilateral systems?

14. What are the functions and limitations of ego-centered groups?

15. Why do descent groups emerge?

16. What functions do kinship terminologies serve?

17. What are the major systems of kinship terminology?

18. What is the main feature of the Eskimo system of descent?

19. What is the simplest descent system? Why is it considered simple?

20. With which type of descent group is Iroquois terminology commonly correlated?

21. How can anthropologists assist Native Americans in their struggles for federal recognition?

Multiple-Choice Practice Questions

1. Descent groups _____.
   a. are composed of those who claim to be lineally descended from a particular ancestor
   b. are common in human societies
   c. trace their connections back to a common ancestor through a chain of parent-child links, and thus appear to stem from the parent-child bond
   d. help provide jobs for their members
   e. "are composed of those who claim to be lineally descended from a particular ancestor", "are common in human societies" and "trace their connections back to a common ancestor through a chain of parent-child links, and thus appear to stem from the parent-child bond"

2. By tracing membership either through males or through females, members of unilineal descent groups _____.

   a. know exactly to which group they belong and where their primary loyalties lie

   b. are confused about their relationship to persons not included in the group

   c. act like females if they are in a matrilineal group

   d. act life males if they are in a patrilineal group

   e. know exactly how many children they are going to have

3. You belong to a patrilineal descent group. Which of the following belong to the same group?

   a. your mother

   b. your father's sister

   c. your mother's sister

   d. your mother's father

   e. your father's sister's children

4. A network of relatives within which individuals possess certain mutual rights and obligations is called _____.

   a. exogamy

   b. descent

   c. kindred

   d. terminology

   e. kinship

5. A boy is born into a society that practices matrilineal descent. The person who exercises authority over him is _____.

   a. his sister

   b. his father

   c. his mother

   d. his mother's brother

   e. his father's sister

6. Among the Yako of Nigeria, an individual might inherit grazing lands from his father's patrilineal group, and livestock and ritual knowledge from his mother's matrilineal group. This is an example of _____ descent.

   a. ambilineal

   b. bilocal

   c. patrilateral

   d. indivisible

   e. double

7. Which of the following kinship systems is most commonly found in the United States?

   a. Eskimo

   b. Hawaiian

c. Iroquois

d. Crow

e. Omaha

8. Descent groups _____.

   a. are economic units providing mutual aid

   b. provide social security for elderly members

   c. often promote solidarity by encouraging worship of the group's ancestors

   d. play a role in deciding appropriate marriage partners

   e. "are economic units providing mutual aid", "provide social security for elderly members", "often promote solidarity by encouraging worship of the group's ancestors" and "play a role in deciding appropriate marriage partners"

9. A lineage is a corporate descent group _____.

   a. the members of which can buy shares in the corporation

   b. the members of which claim descent from a common ancestor

   c. the members of which know the exact genealogical linkages by which they are related to the common ancestor

   d. composed of consanguineal kin

   e. "the members of which claim descent from a common ancestor", "the members of which know the exact genealogical linkages by which they are related to the common ancestor" and "composed of consanguineal kin"

10. A totem _____.

   a. is a word that comes from the Ojibwa American Indian word that means "he is a relative of mine."

   b. is a symbol of animals, plants, natural forces, and objects

   c. is usually associated with a clan's concept of its mythical origins

   d. may be found in our own society in the names we give to baseball and football teams

   e. "is a word that comes from the Ojibwa American Indian word that means 'he is a relative of mine.'", "is a symbol of animals, plants, natural forces, and objects", "is usually associated with a clan's concept of its mythical origins" and "may be found in our own society in the names we give to baseball and football teams"

11. A phratry is a unilineal descent group composed of two or more _____ that believe they are related to each other.

   a. moieties

   b. totems

   c. kindred

   d. lineages

   e. clans

12. Members of a moiety _____.

    a. belong to one of two major descent groups in a society

    b. are those who are divorced (they lack their "better half")

    c. are usually able to trace their exact genealogical links to their common ancestor

    d. feel a much stronger feeling of kinship than is felt by members of a lineage or clan

    e. belong to a group that is smaller than a lineage

13. A person in a system of bilateral descent _____.

    a. traces descent through the father for some purposes and through the mother for other purposes

    b. traces descent through female lines

    c. traces descent through male lines

    d. uses totems to symbolically represent the group

    e. traces descent through both parents simultaneously and recognizes multiple ancestors

14. Descent groups are frequently found to be important organizing devices in _____.

    a. food-foraging societies

    b. horticultural societies

    c. pastoral societies

    d. intensive agricultural societies

    e. horticultural societies, pastoral societies and intensive agricultural societies

15. _____ develop out of extended families when families split up and move to nearby regions, and the core members of these families recognize their descent from a common ancestor and continue to organize activities based on this idea.

    a. Phratries

    b. Kindred groups

    c. Lineages

    d. Moieties

    e. Cognatic groups

16. If two people are given the same kinship term, this means that _____.

    a. they have the same genes

    b. no one can tell the difference between them

    c. they occupy a similar status

    d. they are identical twins

    e. they are members of an adopted family

17. In _____ kinship terminology, ego's "brother" and "sister" are distinguished from "cousins"; both ego's father's brother and mother's brother are given the same kinship term, "uncle."

    a. Eskimo

    b. Hawaiian

    c. Crow

d. Omaha

e. Iroquois

18. In the _____ system of kinship terminology, ego's father, father's brother, and mother's brother are all referred to by the same term, and ego's mother, mother's sister, and father's sister are all referred to by the same term; the term "brother" includes ego's brothers as well as male cousins.
    a. Iroquois
    b. Crow
    c. Omaha
    d. Hawaiian
    e. Eskimo

19. In _____ kinship terminology, the term "brother" is given to ego's brother, father's brother's son, and mother's sister's son; a different term is used for the sons of father's sister and mother's brother. "Mother" refers to ego's mother and mother's sister; "father" refers to ego's father and father's brother. Separate terms are used for ego's mother's brother and father's sister.
    a. Eskimo
    b. Hawaiian
    c. Iroquois
    d. cognatic
    e. kindred

20. Patrilineal descent is also called _____.
    a. bilateral descent
    b. double descent
    c. matrilineal descent
    d. cognitive descent
    e. agnatic descent

21. Honor killings are found among _____ immigrants in the Netherlands.
    a. Canadian
    b. Egyptian
    c. French
    d. Polish
    e. Turkish

22. Which aboriginal group has origin myths of their mythical homeland, Hawaiki?
    a. Hawaiians
    b. Crow
    c. Hopi
    d. Australians
    e. Maori

23. In autumn 1981, Dutch anthropologist _____ went to Maine to check out a job at the Association of Aroostook Indians, which needed a research and development director.
    a. Lewis Henry Morgan
    b. Fred Plog
    c. G. P. Murdock
    d. Weston LaBarre
    e. Harald Prins

24. This British anthropologist defined totemism.
    a. Margaret Mead
    b. Leslie White
    c. Julian Steward
    d. A. R. Radcliffe-Brown
    e. Geoffrey Gorer

25. The production of the world's first "test-tube" baby, in a petri dish outside the womb, without sexual intercourse took place in what year?
    a. 1978
    b. 1965
    c. 1954
    d. 1988
    e. 1995

26. All societies have found some form of family and/or household organization a convenient way to deal with problems all human groups encounter. Which of the following would be problems all human groups face?
    a. how to facilitate economic cooperation between the sexes
    b. when to retire
    c. how to regulate sexual activity
    d. how to provide a proper setting for child rearing
    e. "how to facilitate economic cooperation between the sexes", "how to regulate sexual activity" and "how to provide a proper setting for child rearing"

27. Honor among Turkish immigrants in the Netherlands is called _____.
    a. *iki*
    b. *mana*
    c. *namus*
    d. *hawaiki*
    e. *tapu*

28. Two or more clans together constitute larger units called _____.
    a. moieties
    b. phratries

   c. extended families

   d. blended families

   e. ambilocal clans

29. The descent system that allows each individual the option of affiliating with either the mother's or the father's descent group is known as _____ descent.

   a. double

   b. matrilineal

   c. patrilineal

   d. avunculocal

   e. ambilineal

30. Which of the following groups is a matrilineal society?

   a. Yanomamo

   b. Chinese

   c. Hopi

   d. Iroquois

   e. Yako

31. The _____, like Microsoft and Intel, is a corporate group.

   a. lineage

   b. clan

   c. clique

   d. cousin club

   e. fraternity

32. In some cultures, lineages facing exceptional challenges to their survival may choose to ritually adopt individuals not related by birth. Such was the case among the _____ in the 17th and 18th centuries.

   a. Apache

   b. Iroquois

   c. Lakota

   d. Chumash

   e. Onandaga

33. The kin-ordered social structure of the Winnebago Indian nation offers an interesting ethnographic example of a _____ system.

   a. lineage

   b. clan

   c. phratry

   d. moiety

   e. ambilocal

34. Which of the following is **not** a lineage system?

    a. matrilineal

    b. patrilineal

    c. unilineal

    d. trifurcated

    e. bilateral

35. Patriclans trace descent exclusively through men from a founding ancestor. Historically, a few dozen of such clans existed in the _____.

    a. Torey Islands

    b. Guatemalan Highlands

    c. Canadian provinces

    d. Australian Outback

    e. Scottish Highlands

True/False Practice Questions

1. Cross-cousins are ideal marriage partners in an arrangement whereby lineages engage in reciprocal marriage exchanges to establish alliances.
   True or False

2. Ambilineal descent is a form of double descent.
   True or False

3. The kindred is a kin group that is organized laterally rather than lineally.
   True or False

4. The boundaries of a kindred are permanent and definite.
   True or False

5. Samoan Islanders practice unilineal descent.
   True or False

6. Turkish immigrants to the Netherlands continue to hold some of their traditional customs.
   True or False

7. Bilateral descent exists in various foraging cultures.
   True or False

8. All kinship terminologies classify similar individuals into similar categories.
   True or False

9. Euroamericans commonly use the Iroquois system of kinship.
   True or False

10. Among the Han Chinese residence is matrilocal.
    True or False

11. Among the Hopi residence is patrilocal.
    True or False

12. The Maori are a group of aborigines in New Zealand.
    True or False

13. Unilineal descent provides an easy way of restricting descent group membership to minimize problems of divided loyalty and the like.
    True or False

14. Bilateral kinship and bilateral descent cannot be used interchangeably since they have different meanings.
    True or False

15. Descent groups do not need to clearly define membership to operate efficiently.
    True or False

16. In a society where descent is traced patrilineally, maternal relatives are less important.
    True or False

17. Double descent, whereby descent is reckoned both patrilineally and matrilineally at the same time, is very rare.
    True or False

18. Because of its bilateral structure, a kindred is never the same for any two persons except siblings. Thus, no two people (except siblings) belong to the same kindred.
    True or False

19. Each Scottish clan has its own traditional tartan, the patterns themselves are extremely ancient.
    True or False

20. The traditional Scottish tartans are a colorful symbol of a shared heritage between even very distant relatives living very far apart.
    True or False

21. It is now possible for a woman to give birth to her genetic uncle.
    True or False

Practice Short Answer Questions

1. Describe the kin-ordered social structure of the Winnebago Indian nation.

2. Explain why Scottish clans continue to survive.

3. What is meant by "new reproductive techniques (NRT)?"

4. Due to "new reproductive techniques (NRT)," it has been suggested that at least ten different terms are needed to cover the concepts of "mother" and "father" in Western societies. Identify those suggested terms.

5. Explain the difference between clan, clan, phratry, and moiety.

6. What are the three primary kinship systems?

7. What are the differences between a matrilineal and patrilineal society?

8. How can anthropologists work to help immigrants better adapt to their new lives?

Practice Essays

1. Compare and contrast the social organization of the Hopi and the Chinese.

2. Many North American feminists are interested in the concept of matriarchy, sometimes confusing it with or linking it to the matrilineal descent system. Does matrilineality imply matriarchy? Use concrete examples to explore this.

3. Describe a typical woman's life among the Han Chinese.

4. Discuss the inevitable changes that will have to occur with traditional notions of kinship and gender, due to the advent of new reproductive technologies that separate conception from birth and eggs from wombs.

5. Descent groups are convenient devices for solving a number of problems human societies commonly confront. Identify the problems and describe how a descent group solves them.

6. Discuss the forms and functions of descent groups.

7. The culture's descent system is closely tied to a society's economic base. Explain why this is so.

8. How do kinship terms reflect life in a society?

Solutions

Multiple-Choice Practice Questions

1. E
2. A
3. B
4. E
5. D
6. E
7. A
8. E
9. E
10. E
11. E
12. A
13. E
14. E
15. C
16. C
17. A
18. D
19. C
20. E
21. E
22. E
23. E
24. D
25. A
26. E
27. C
28. B
29. E
30. C
31. A
32. B
33. D
34. D
35. E

True/False Practice Questions

1. T
2. F
3. T
4. F
5. F
6. T
7. T
8. T
9. F
10. F
11. F
12. T
13. T
14. T
15. F
16. F
17. T
18. T
19. F
20. T
21. T

Chapter 11

Grouping by Gender, Age, Common Interest, and Class

Synopsis

Challenge Issues: What principles do people use to organize societies? What is age grading? What are common-interest associations? What is social stratification? This chapter examines major kinds of non-kin organizations. Groups defined by gender, age, common interest, and class are described, as are various degrees of social mobility found in stratified societies. Stratified forms of social organization such as those involving class or caste are presented in the conclusion of the chapter.

Chapter Objectives

   I.   grouping by gender

   II.   grouping by age

   III.   grouping by common interest

   IV.   grouping by class or social rank in stratified societies

Key Terms

age grade	egalitarian societies
age set	social class
caste	social mobility
common-interest associations	stratified societies

Exercises

The Anthropology Resource Center (ARC)

The Anthropology Resource Center is a dynamic, subfield-specific website that provides a wealth of materials for both students and instructors to reinforce key concepts in anthropology. All of the resources and activities encourage students to apply anthropology beyond the textbook and classroom. ARC can be reached through the weblink http://thomsonedu.com/. After selecting the discipline of "Anthropology" under "Humanities and Social Sciences," go directly to ARC for a wide range of resources that bring anthropology to life through pictures, interviews, news items, interactive displays, maps, and more. (This site is passcode-protected for both instructors and students.)

Review Questions

1. Describe the separate but equal organization of the Iroquois.

2. In what ways is age grouping evidenced in North America?

3. How does one become a member of an age grade?

4. Distinguish between an age group and an age set.

5. Describe the Tiriki age-set system.

6. How and why are common-interest associations formed?

7. Historically, why have women's groups been less common than men's?

8. What functions do women's associations have?

9. What purposes do urban-oriented associations serve?

10. Describe the interstrata relationship in a stratified society.

11. Contrast an egalitarian society with a stratified society.

12. In what ways might a society be stratified?

13. Briefly describe India's caste system.

14. How might a stratified society beget an outcast group?

15. What are three aspects of a social-class structure?

16. Distinguish between the three ways social class are manifest in society.

17. What is social-impact assessment?

18. What role does religion play in India's caste system?

19. What were the findings of the African Burial Project?

20. What are "virtual" common-interest associations?

Fill-in-the-Blank

1. An age _____ is a category based on age, a stage through which people pass (such as a "teenager").
2. An age _____ is a group of people who move through life stages together (such as "baby boomers").
3. Among the _____ of South America, men and women work, eat, and sleep separately.
4. Common-interest associations used to be called _____ associations.
5. The text suggests that the caste system is present not only in India but also in _____, _____ and _____.
6. A _____ society is one in which members do not share equally in prestige and basic resources.
7. _____ is a special form of social class in which membership is determined by birth and remains fixed for life.
8. In a class society, people are theoretically able to change their class positions through social _____.

Multiple-Choice Practice Questions

1. High rates of rape appear to be associated with societies in which the roles of males and females are highly segregated, and in which there are efforts by males to be dominant over women. If this is true, we would expect the highest rate of rape to occur among the _____.

   a. Ju/'hoansi
   b. Mundurucu
   c. Iroquois
   d. Mbuti
   e. Hopi

2. In literate societies that rely on the written word for accumulated wisdom, elders are often _____.

   a. treated with great respect because of their wisdom
   b. considered to be as valuable as their weight in gold
   c. treated like "living libraries" that contain much needed knowledge
   d. not considered sources of information
   e. killed when they turn sixty-five years old

3. The following _____ are passed through by members of North American culture: toddler, teenager, senior citizen.

   a. age grades
   b. age sets
   c. social classes
   d. castes
   e. open classes

4. Which of the following statements about common-interest associations is **incorrect**?

   a. they were originally referred to in the anthropological literature as voluntary associations
   b. common-interest associations are more common in hunter-gatherer societies than in urban-industrial societies
   c. common-interest associations are intimately associated with world urbanization and increasing social complexity
   d. common-interest associations are found in many traditional societies
   e. sometimes one can join a common-interest association voluntarily, and sometimes membership is required by law

5. The text suggests that women's participation in common-interest associations in traditional societies is often less than men's because _____.
   a. women are less sociable than men
   b. women have no interests in common because they see each other as sexual competitors
   c. women remain at home, isolated from other women
   d. men prevent women from joining such groupings
   e. women have so many opportunities to socialize that they have little need for common-interest associations.

6. In times of rapid social change _____.
   a. common-interest associations decline in significance
   b. common-interest associations assume the roles and functions formerly held by kinship or age groups
   c. women form common-interest associations whereas men retain their membership in age and kinship groups
   d. men are able to adapt whereas women are not
   e. the role of the elderly becomes more important as the society adjusts to change

7. A society composed of several groups that differ in their access to resources and prestige is said to be _____.
   a. stratified
   b. unfair
   c. immoral
   d. egalitarian
   e. open

8. A/An _____ is a special form of social class in which membership is determined by birth and remains fixed for life.
   a. clan
   b. phratry
   c. common-interest association
   d. age group
   e. caste

9. Symbolic indicators may not always be reliable in helping you assess someone's class status. Which of the following is an example of this?
   a. a common form of recreation of lower-class males is playing pool at the local beer joint
   b. a con man from a lower-class background wears a tuxedo when he tries to sell you shares in a nonexistent corporation
   c. according to Emily Post, one can always identify upper-crust families by the presence of a day maid

d. Demille O'Hara, striving to return to the simplicity of life as lived by his tribal ancestors, lets his day maid go

e. a con man from a lower-class background wears a tuxedo when he "tries to sell you shares in a nonexistent corporation," "Demille O'Hara, striving to return to the simplicity of life as lived by his tribal ancestors, lets his day maid go"

10. The ability to change one's class position is known as _____.

a. open class

b. egalitarian

c. social mobility

d. indicative of common-interest societies

e. inevitable

11. The degree of social mobility in a stratified society is related to _____.

a. the prevailing kind of family organization

b. its ideology

c. the number of different common-interest associations it has

d. the difference between its richest and poorest classes

e. genetic factors

12. Which of the following could have contributed to the emergence of social stratification?

a. All human beings want to be looked up to by their fellow members of society.

b. Certain descent groups may have monopolized activities that turned out to play an important role in their society (such as propitiation of the gods in a horticultural society exposed to unpredictable weather).

c. An ethnic group with an economic or military advantage (such as knowledge of intensive agriculture or possession of firearms) that enters a foreign territory may become the ruling class within that area.

d. "All human beings want to be looked up to by their fellow members of society," "certain descent groups may have monopolized activities that turned out to play an important role in their society (such as propitiation of the gods in a horticultural society exposed to unpredictable weather)" and "an ethnic group with an economic or military advantage (such as knowledge of intensive agriculture or possession of firearms) that enters a foreign territory may become the ruling class within that area."

e. none of these

13. A kind of policy research frequently done by an anthropologist is called a _____.

a. ethnology

b. ethnography

c. participant observation

d. social impact assessment

e. needs assessment

14. In the U.S., any project requiring a federal permit or licence, or using federal funds, by law must be preceded by a _____.

   a. needs assessment

   b. archaeological assessment

   c. cultural impact assessment

   d. assessment of feasibility

   e. social impact statement

15. Anthropologist _____ was hired to carry out a social impact assessment of a water diversion project in New Mexico.

   a. Sue Ellen Jacobs

   b. Harald Prins

   c. R. M. Bradfield

   d. P. R. Sanday

   e. Fred Plog

16. What the term _____ really refers to are those associations not based on sex, age, kinship, marriage, or territory that result from an act of joining.

   a. clan

   b. age grade

   c. voluntary association

   d. neighborhood association

   e. women's auxiliary

17. Which of the following is not an example of a common-interest organization?

   a. the American Federation of Labor

   b. the National Rifle Association

   c. the Navajo Nation

   d. the Aryan Nation

   e. the Green Party

18. Which of the following would be reasons for the decline in membership in common-interest associations in the United States?

   a. viewing television

   b. frequent moves

   c. long working hours

   d. the Internet

   e. viewing television, frequent moves, long working hours and the Internet

19. Social scientists have observed that today, with outright unemployment at historically low levels, the _____ provides a pool of cheap labor.

   a. lower castes

   b. middle-class

c. underclass

d. mentally-challenged

e. pariah groups

20. In which of the following societies are men and women rigidly segregated in what they do?

a. Seneca

b. Oneida

c. Mohawk

d. Onondaga

e. Seneca, Oneida, Mohawk and Onondaga

21. Age grouping is so familiar and so important that it and _____ sometimes have been called the only universal factors for determining a person's position in society.

a. height

b. weight

c. eye color

d. sex

e. shoe size

22. The members of a/an _____ usually remain closely associated throughout their lives, or at least most of their lives.

a. fraternity

b. sorority

c. union

d. kindred

e. age set

23. All stratified societies offer at least some _____, and this helps to ease the strains in any system of inequality.

a. stability

b. reliability

c. instability

d. mobility

e. shakiness

24. In which of the following ways are societies stratified?

a. gender

b. age

c. social class

d. caste

e. gender, age, social class and caste

25. The highest caste in the Indian system is the _____caste.
    a. Harijan
    b. Brahmans
    c. Vaisyas
    d. Shudras
    e. Kshatriyas

26. The fighters and rulers in the Indian system come from the _____ caste.
    a. Shudras
    b. Harijan
    c. Vaisyas
    d. Brahman
    e. Kshatriyas

27. In the Indian system, those members of the Vaisyas caste are the _____.
    a. fighters and rulers.
    b. merchants and traders.
    c. artisans and laborers.
    d. "untouchables."
    e. priests and lawgivers.

28. The artists and laborers are members of the _____ caste in the Indian system.
    a. Shudras
    b. Harijan
    c. Vaisyas
    d. Brahmans
    e. Kshatriyas

29. In which of the following countries might a caste-like system be found?
    a. Canada
    b. France
    c. Italy
    d. Bolivia
    e. Argentina

30. A caste-like system based on skin color and wealth once existed in _____ where a white minority created a political regime Apartheid.
    a. Germany
    b. Holland
    c. Belgium
    d. Sudan
    e. South Africa

31. The director of the African Burial Ground Project was biological anthropologist
    _____.

    a. Jennifer Thompson.
    b. Victoria Cassman
    c. Sheila Brooks
    d. Michael Blakey
    e. Summer Decker

True/False Practice Questions

1. Division of labor by sex is characteristic of all human societies.
   True or False

2. Usually an increase in the number of common-interest associations is associated with urbanization, but these associations are also found in traditional societies.
   True or False

3. Castes are strongly exogamous.
   True or False

4. Mobility refers to the ability to change one's class position.
   True or False

5. An age grade is a group of people initiated into the group at the same time who move though the series of categories together.
   True or False

6. One of the major objections to the construction of the water diversion project in New Mexico is that it would result in the obliteration of the three-hundred-year-old irrigation system structures.
   True or False

7. Observers have noted a recent decrease in participation in all sorts of common-interest associations.
   True or False

8. According to Mundurucu beliefs men have always ruled over women.
   True or False

9. Like age grades, age sets cease to exist after a specified number of years.
   True or False

10. Common-interest associations have proliferated modern society, but are not found in many traditional societies.
    True or False

11. The Indian caste system has absolutely no flexibility and/or mobility.
    True or False

12. A caste-like system could never have existed in the United States.
    True or False

13. Individuals born and raised within large-scale societies face the challenge of succeeding within a complex social structure that extends well beyond kinship.
    True or False

14. India's national constitution of 1950 abolished caste discrimination and the practice of untouchability, in effect doing away with the caste system.
    True or False

Practice Matching

Match the culture with its characteristic.

1. _____ Iroquois
2. _____ Tiriki
3. _____ South Africans
4. _____ Mundurucu
5. _____ Apsarok (Crow) Indians

a. African nomadic pastoralists with an age set/age grade system
b. Castelike social organization based on racial divisions
c. Native Americans with separate but equal gender organization
d. group in the Brazilian rainforest that have disharmonious relations between the sexes
e. Women were allowed to participate in the secret Tobacco Society

Practice Short Answer Questions

1. Discuss India's untouchables and their plight.

2. What is the "one drop" rule?

3. Under what conditions does social stratification become a problem?

4. What is grouping by age? Provide examples.

5. What is grouping by gender? Provide examples.

6. What is the significance of the Jewish *eruv*?

7. Distinguish between class and caste.

8. How does Swaziland exhibit characteristics of a state?

9. What is social mobility and how does it function?

10. What is significant about the work of the African Burial Project?

Practice Essays

1. Marx felt that religion was "the opiate of the masses," claiming that it was often used by the upper classes to perpetuate their own dominance. Can this perspective be applied to the Indian caste system? Would it be ethnocentric to do so?

2. What were the findings of the social impact assessment of the water diversion project in New Mexico?

3. Although important differences exist, there are nonetheless interesting similarities between Mundurucu beliefs and those of traditional European culture. Discuss those similarities.

4. Compare and contrast stratified societies with egalitarian societies.

5. Some observers have noted a recent decline in participation in all types of common-interest organizations, at least in North America. What is the explanation for this decline? Explain.

6. The classic ethnographic example of a caste system is the Hindu caste system of India. Describe that system.

7. Discuss the caste-like social system called Apartheid that was established in South Africa.

8. Describe how social classes make life oppressive for large numbers of people, while at the same time performing an integrative function in society.

9. What were the findings of the African Burial Ground Project?

Solutions

Fill-in-the-Blank

1. grade
2. set
3. Mundurucu
4. voluntary
5. South Africa, the U.S., China
6. stratified
7. A caste
8. mobility

Multiple-Choice Practice Questions

1. B
2. D
3. A
4. B
5. E
6. B
7. A
8. E
9. E
10. C
11. A
12. D
13. D
14. E
15. A
16. C
17. C
18. E
19. C
20. E
21. D
22. E
23. D
24. E
25. B
26. E
27. B
28. A
29. D
30. E
31. D

True/False Practice Questions

1. T
2. T
3. F
4. T
5. F
6. T
7. T
8. F
9. F
10. F
11. F
12. F
13. T
14. F

Practice Matching

1. C
2. A
3. B
4. D
5. E

Chapter 12

Politics, Power, and Violence

Synopsis

Challenge Issues: How are power and political organization different? How are social and political organization formed and maintained? How do political systems obtain popular support? This chapter begins by noting that all social relations involve power, "the ability of individuals or groups to impose their will upon others." The authors define political organization as "the way power is distributed and embedded in society." Describing four basic kinds of political systems, they discuss types of political leaders, religion, gender and politics, and the maintenance of order cross-culturally. The authors define "law" in cross-cultural terms.

Chapter Objectives

    I.   kinds of political systems

   II.   political systems and the question of legitimacy

  III.   politics and religion

  IV.   political leadership and gender

   V.   political organization and the maintenance of order

  VI.   social control through law

 VII.   violent conflict and warfare

Key Terms

adjudication

band

chiefdom

cultural control

law

legitimacy

mediation

nation

negotiation

political organization

power

sanction

social control

state

tribe

Exercises

The Anthropology Resource Center (ARC)

The Anthropology Resource Center is a dynamic, subfield-specific website that provides a wealth of materials for both students and instructors to reinforce key concepts in anthropology. All of the resources and activities encourage students to apply anthropology beyond the textbook and classroom. ARC can be reached through the weblink http://thomsonedu.com/. After selecting the discipline of "Anthropology" under "Humanities and Social Sciences," go directly to ARC for a wide range of resources that bring anthropology to life through pictures, interviews, news items, interactive displays, maps, and more. (This site is passcode-protected for both instructors and students.)

Review Questions

1. What are the four basic kinds of political systems?

2. What kinds of societies typically have uncentralized systems?

3. How is authority conferred in a band?

4. How is authority conferred in a tribe?

5. What is the function of age-grade systems in the political structure of tribes?

6. Describe the role of the *tonowi* among the Kapauku Papuans.

7. What kinds of societies typically have centralized political systems?

8. Distinguish between nation and state.

9. What has women's role generally been in political leadership?

10. Describe women's role in Igbo society.

11. How is social control generally maintained in bands and tribes?

12. How do internalized controls guide behavior?

13. Distinguish between positive and negative sanctions.

14. Distinguish between informal and formal sanctions.

15. Why is the definition of law destined to be inexact?

16. What are the functions of law?

17. Differentiate between negotiation, adjudication, and mediation.

18. How are disputes handled by the Kpelle?

19. Why might warfare be so prominent in food-producing societies?

20. How did the Aztec worldview contribute to the incidence of warfare in their society?

21. Distinguish between force and legitimacy.

22. In what ways is religion connected with politics?

23. What does the term *political organization* refer to?

24. Identify three groups of people, and the area where they live, who do not practice warfare as we know it.

Fill-in-the-Blank

1. The term _____ refers to the system of social relationships that is connected with the maintenance of public order.

2. Tribal population densities may be as high as _____ people per square mile.

3. Anthropologists have identified four types of political systems; two are said to be _____ and two are _____.

169

4. An egalitarian, autonomous small group composed of related people who occupy a single region is called a _____.

5. All humans were food foragers living in band-type organizations until about _____ years ago.

6. The _____ are an example of a society practicing band-level organization.

7. Most conflict in bands is settled by informal means, and decisions are usually made by _____.

8. A _____ is a larger grouping than a band and is linked to a specific territory.

9. The Kpelle are ruled by a _____.

10. The smallest unit of the Swazi government was the _____.

11. In tribal societies of Melanesia, a type of leader called the _____ or *tonowi* is prevalent.

12. A _____ is a ranked society in which every member has a position in the hierarchy.

13. Chiefdoms are linked to _____ economic systems.

14. The Swazi have a _____-level political system.

15. States are typically linked to _____ subsistence patterns.

16. An example of a society in which women play a notably strong political role is the _____.

17. The Wape of New Guinea use belief in _____ as a means of social control.

18. In North America we rely on both external and _____ controls to maintain social order.

19. The Inuit use _____ as a means of resolving conflict.

20. Western societies make a distinction between _____ law, involving offenses committed against individuals, and _____ law, involving offenses committed against the state.

21. Disputes may be settled by _____, the use of direct argument and compromise by the disputing parties, or by _____, settlement through the assistance of an unbiased third party.

22. Warfare is most closely linked to the _____-type political system.

Multiple-Choice Practice Questions

1. Power can be defined as _____.
   a. a form of strength administered by chiefdoms and states
   b. military force used in situations of warfare internationally only
   c. aggressive force associated exclusively with centralized organizations
   d. the institution of violence upon the individual or group
   e. the ability of individuals or groups to impose their will upon others

2. Bands and tribes are both _____.
   a. centralized
   b. associated with industrialism
   c. dependent on age groups for political organization
   d. uncentralized and egalitarian
   e. hierarchical in social organization

3. The form of social organization typical of hunter-gatherers is the _____, whereas horticulture and pastoralism are usually associated with the form of social organization called the
   _____.
   a. tribe/chiefdom
   b. tribe/state
   c. tribe/band
   d. band/chiefdom
   e. band/tribe

4. Queen Pomare IV was the leader of the chiefdom of _____.
   a. Kapauku
   b. Kpelle
   c. Samoa
   d. Tahiti
   e. Melanesia

5. Age-grade systems and common-interest associations are effective methods of integrating small autonomous units such as bands into larger social units. These methods may be described as _____ systems of political organization.
   a. segmentary
   b. negotiated
   c. state
   d. nonkinship
   e. kinship

6. A _____ is a ranked society in which every member has a position in the hierarchy, and an individual's status is determined by membership in a descent group.
   a. band
   b. tribe
   c. chiefdom
   d. state
   e. kindred

7. The state is distinctive in the extensiveness of its legitimate use of _____ to regulate the affairs of its citizens.
    a. kinship
    b. force
    c. chiefs
    d. religion
    e. gossip

8. In a chiefdom, an individual's status is determined by membership in a _____.
    a. government
    b. social class
    c. bureaucracy
    d. descent group
    e. secret society

9. A cross-cultural comparison of systems of political organization reveals that _____.
    a. many women who hold high office do so by virtue of their relationship to men
    b. many women in positions of leadership adopt characteristics of temperament that are usually considered masculine
    c. in a number of societies, women have as much political power as men
    d. women may play an important role in political decisions even when they are not visible public leaders
    e. "many women who hold high office do so by virtue of their relationship to men," "many women in positions of leadership adopt characteristics of temperament that are usually considered masculine," "in a number of societies, women have as much political power as men," and "women may play an important role in political decisions even when they are not visible public leaders"

10. At the heart of political organization is _____.
    a. control of unacceptable social behavior
    b. the legitimate use of force to maintain order
    c. unequal access to power
    d. the dominance of males over females
    e. the development of egalitarian relationships

11. Sanctions refer to _____.
    a. internalized social controls
    b. holy behavior
    c. externalized social controls
    d. decadent behavior
    e. ritualized behavior

12. _____ sanctions attempt to precisely and explicitly regulate people's behavior. They can be positive (such as military decorations) or negative (such as imprisonment).

    a. Hierarchical
    b. Egalitarian
    c. Informal
    d. Formal
    e. Magical

13. In centralized societies, antisocial behavior is usually dealt with in a court system by the use of formal, negative sanctions involving the application of abstract rules and the use of force. The primary aim is _____.

    a. to help the victim
    b. to renew social relations between the victim and the perpetrator of the crime
    c. to prevent witchcraft from being used
    d. to assign and punish guilt
    e. to provide a good show for the spectators

14. The functions of law include _____.

    a. the definition of proper behavior in particular circumstances so that everyone is clear about their rights and duties
    b. protecting the wealthy from the poor
    c. redefining what is proper behavior when situations change
    d. allocating authority to use coercion to enforce sanctions
    e. "the definition of proper behavior in particular circumstances so that everyone is clear about their rights and duties," "redefining what is proper behavior when situations change," and "allocating authority to use coercion to enforce sanctions"

15. A method of resolving disputes in which the disputing parties voluntarily arrive at a mutually satisfactory agreement is called _____.

    a. negotiation
    b. mediation
    c. adjudication
    d. use of sanctions
    e. law

16. Which of the following are likely to be associated with warfare?

    a. centralized political systems
    b. the rise of cities
    c. a technology that supports population growth
    d. possession of complex, valuable property
    e. "centralized political systems," "the rise of cities," "a technology that supports population growth," and "possession of complex, valuable property"

17. An exploitative world view is more likely to exist in which of the following technologies?
    a. food foraging
    b. horticulture
    c. pastoralism
    d. intensive agriculture
    e. horticulture, pastoralism and intensive agriculture

18. Power based on force does not usually last very long; to be effective, it must be considered _____.
    a. legitimate
    b. mediated
    c. negotiated
    d. subject to sanctions
    e. inevitable

19. The *obi* and *omu* were part of _____ society.
    a. Kapauku
    b. Navajo
    c. Algonquian
    d. Aztec
    e. Igbo

20. Another agent of control in societies, whether or not they possess centralized political systems, may be _____.
    a. witchcraft
    b. sorcerers
    c. ostracism
    d. fines set by judges
    e. warriors

21. An important pioneer in the anthropological study of law was _____.
    a. A. L. Kroeber
    b. George Peter Murdock
    c. John Wesley Powell
    d. E. Adamson Hoebel
    e. Peggy Reeves Sanday

22. The field of _____ is one of growing anthropological involvement and employment.
    a. ethnoscience
    b. ethnology
    c. dispute control
    d. dispute management
    e. assertiveness training

23. In 1980 _____, as a practitioner of dispute management, helped the U.S. and the Soviet Union replace their obsolete "hot line" with fully equipped nuclear crisis centers in each capital.
    a. Sue Ellen Jacobs
    b. William L. Ury
    c. Laura Nader
    d. L. Abu-Lughod
    e. Harald Prins

24. When one refers to the way power is distributed and embedded in society, one is referring to a society's _____.
    a. social organization
    b. military structure
    c. political ideology
    d. class structure
    e. political organization

25. The ability to control others' behavior, whether organizing a seal hunt or raising a military force, has to do with the way power is distributed and embedded in a society, or its _____.
    a. political organization
    b. social class structure
    c. political ideology
    d. police force
    e. social system

26. To support the view that humans are innately warlike observers cite the behavior of people such as the _____, who are portrayed as living in a constant state of war.
    a. Apache
    b. Comanche
    c. Ju/'hoansi
    d. Mende
    e. Yanomami

27. It is clear that war is not a universal phenomenon, for in various parts of the world there are societies that do not practice warfare as we know it. Which of the following groups of people is **not** an example of a group that does not practice warfare?
    a. the Bushman of southern Africa
    b. the Arapesh of New Guinea
    c. the Hopi of the American southwest
    d. the Yanomami of South America
    e. all are warlike; the Bushman of southern Africa, the Arapesh of New Guinea, the Hopi of the American southwest and the Yanomami of South America

28. Scholars have identified four basic kinds of political systems and categorized them into uncentralized and centralized. Which of the following would be considered uncentralized systems?

    a. chiefdoms

    b. tribes

    c. states

    d. bands

    e. tribes and bands

29. The _____ do not think of government as something fixed and all-powerful, and to them leadership was not vested in a central authority.

    a. Navajo

    b. Melanesians

    c. Mayan

    d. Yanomami

    e. Gururumba

30. The Beaver Wars involved all of the following groups except the _____.

    a. Oneida

    b. Navajo

    c. Mohawk

    d. Seneca

    e. Onondaga

31. _____ systems provide a tribal society with a means of political integration beyond the kin group.

    a. Age-grade

    b. Common-interest association

    c. Segmentary lineage

    d. Kindred

    e. Clan

32. An important pioneer in the anthropological study of law was _____.

    a. E. E. Evans-Pritchard

    b. Marshall Sahlins

    c. Leo Pospisil

    d. E. Adamson Hoebel

    e. A. R. Radcliffe-Brown

33. Although leaders of chiefdoms are almost always men, in some cultures a politically astute wife, sister, or single daughter of a deceased male chief could inherit that position. One historical example is Queen _____ who succeeded her half brother as leader of the Polynesian chiefdom of Tahiti in 1827.

    a. Liliokalnai

    b. Latifah

c. Wilhelmina

d. Pomare IV

e. Isabella

34. _____ is a new state that was formed after an armed struggle with Yugoslavia.

a. Suriname

b. Bosnia

c. Croatia

d. East Timor

e. Kurdistan

35. Some nations have forged their own states without open violence, such was the case with _____.

a. Papua New Guinea

b. Belize

c. Curacao

d. Guyana

e. Trinidad

36. In the past 5,000 years or so, there have been more than _____ wars, resulting in many hundreds of millions of casualties.

a. 1,000

b. 5,000

c. 14,000

d. 20,000

e. 12,000

37. Many armies around the world recruit children. Today, there are more than _____ child soldiers, many as young as 12–15 years-old.

a. 25,000

b. 100,000

c. 250,000

d. 1,000,000

e. 50,000

38. Playing a leading role in the development of the anthropology of law, _____ has taken on specialists in the fields of law, children's issues, nuclear energy, and science, critically questioning the basic assumptions under which these experts operate.

a. Ralph Nader

b. Margaret Mead

c. Martha Knack

d. Laura Nader

e. Ruth Benedict

True/False Practice Questions

1. Negative sanctions are called laws if they are formalized.
    True or False

2. Until recently many non-Western peoples had no fixed form of government in the sense that Westerners understand the term.
    True or False

3. The Ju/'hoansi have a tribal-type political organization.
    True or False

4. The Big Man of the Kapauku is called *tonowi.*
    True or False

5. Chiefdoms and states both have luxury goods available for certain groups of people.
    True or False

6. In many tribal societies the organizing unit is the clan.
    True or False

7. The *tonowi* acquires political power through his loans.
    True or False

8. Typically, chiefdoms involve reciprocal exchange systems.
    True or False

9. A form of settlement that involves a third party is called mediation.
    True or False

10. Between 1975 and 1979, Khmer Rouge murdered some 20 percent of Cambodia's population.
    True or False

11. The challenge of eliminating warfare has never been greater than today.
    True or False

12. What anthropologists involved with dispute management are trying to do is to help create a culture of negotiation in a world where adversarial, win-lose attitudes are out of step with the increasingly interdependent relations between people.
    True or False

13. The term political organization refers to the way power is distributed and embedded in society.
    True or False

14. It is clear that war is a universal phenomenon.
    True or False

15. Among food foragers, with their uncentralized political systems, warfare is all but unknown.
    True or False

16. Among the Igbo of Midwestern Nigeria, women were not allowed positions in the administrative hierarchy.
    True or False

17. Western societies do not clearly distinguish offenses against the state, called crimes, from offenses against individuals, called torts.
True or False

18. Every society develops customs designed to encourage conformity to social norms.
True or False

19. To a greater or lesser extent, political organizations all over the world seek to legitimize their power through recourse to supernatural ideas.
True or False

20. Many contemporary wars are not between states but often occur within countries where the government is either corrupt, ineffective, or without popular support.
True or False

Practice Matching

1. _____ Azande
2. _____ Swazi
3. _____ Igbo
4. _____ Wape
5. _____ Abenaki

a. Nigerian society in which men and women occupy separate political spheres
b. northeastern Native American foragers in the historic past that lived in harmony with their environment
c. a southeast African nation
d. a New Guinea people in the historical past with effective informal and internalized controls
e. a group in the Sudan that practices witchcraft

Short Answer

1. Why is it incorrect to blame political unrest in many parts of the world on "tribalism?"

2. Identify the countries where women have recently been elected and served as presidents or prime ministers.

3. The "Beaver Wars" took place during the 16th century in the American northeast. Explain why they occurred.

4. Explain how the Iroquois Confederacy came into being.

5. Explain formal and informal sanctions.

6. What is witchcraft and how does it contribute to social control of humans societies?

7. What is the evolution of warfare?

8. What is legitimacy and how does affect authority and power?

9. Compare and contrast the tribe and band as institutions of political organization.

Practice Essays

1. Why has the state-type system expanded to encompass most of the globe today? Explore how band, tribe, and chiefdom organizations might persist within a world order based primarily on states.

2. Discuss the impact of Darwin's theory of sexual selection.

3. Who is William L. Ury? What is his area of expertise? What is he trying to accomplish?

4. What is restorative justice and conflict resolution?

5. Why do wars occur? Is the need to wage war an instinctive feature of the human personality? Explain.

6. One of the state's responsibilities is the organization and execution of war. Explain why states revert to war.

7. Describe the Aztec wars and the Christian Crusades and discuss the motivations and justifications for the aggressive behavior of those two groups.

8. What is the relationship between gender and politics?

Solutions

Fill-in-the-Blank

1. political organization
2. 250
3. uncentralized, centralized
4. band
5. 10,000
6. Ju/'hoansi
7. consensus
8. tribe
9. paramount chief
10. homestead
11. Big Man
12. chiefdom
13. redistributive
14. state
15. intensive
16. Iroquois
17. ghosts
18. internal
19. song duels
20. criminal, civil
21. negotiation, mediation
22. state

Multiple-Choice Practice Questions

3. E
4. D
5. D
6. C
7. B
8. D
9. E
10. A
11. C
12. D
13. D
14. E
15. A
16. E
17. E
18. A
19. E
20. A
21. D
22. D
23. B
24. E
25. A
26. E
27. D
28. E
29. A
30. B
31. A
32. D
33. D
34. B
35. A
36. C
37. C
38. D

True/False Practice Questions

1. T
2. T
3. F
4. T
5. T
6. T
7. T
8. F
9. T
10. T
11. T
12. T
13. T
14. F
15. T
16. F
17. F
18. T
19. T
20. T

Practice Matching

1. E
2. C
3. A
4. D
5. B

Chapter 13

Spirituality, Religion, and the Supernatural

Synopsis

Challenge Issues: What are religion and spirituality? What are identifying features of religion and spirituality? What functions do religion and spirituality serve? This chapter discusses the universality of religion, considering the functions served by religious belief and ritual in the social order. The authors compare various kinds of supernatural beings and the relationships among magic, science, and religion. The role of religion in culture change is also explored.

Chapter Objectives

    I.   the anthropological approach to religion

   II.   the practice of religion

  III.   rituals and ceremonies

  IV.   magic

   V.   witchcraft

  VI.   the functions of religion

 VII.   religion and culture change: revitalization movements

Key Terms

animatism	priest or priestess
animism	religion
cargo cults	revitalization movements
contagious magic	rites of intensification
divination	rites of passage
imitative magic	separation
incorporation	transition
pantheon	witchcraft
polytheism	worldview

Exercises

The Anthropology Resource Center (ARC)

The Anthropology Resource Center is a dynamic, subfield-specific website that provides a wealth of materials for both students and instructors to reinforce key concepts in anthropology. All of the resources and activities encourage students to apply anthropology beyond the textbook and classroom. ARC can be reached through the weblink http://thomsonedu.com/. After selecting the discipline of "Anthropology" under "Humanities and Social Sciences," go directly to ARC for a wide range of resources that bring anthropology to life through pictures, interviews, news items, interactive displays, maps, and more. (This site is passcode-protected for both instructors and students.)

Review Questions

1. What is the relationship between religion and spirituality?

2. Why might there be less religion, as defined in your textbook, in more complex societies?

3. What are supernatural beings?

4. What is the role of gods and goddesses in many societies?

5. How does healing occur among the Ju/'hoansi?

6. What purpose do ancestral spirits serve?

7. In what type of society is one likely to find animism?

8. Distinguish between animism and animatism.

9. Where do sacred places tend to be located?

10. In what type of society is one likely to find priestesses?

11. How are shamans made and how do they carry out their work?

12. What benefits do people derive from enlisting the services of a shaman?

13. What are two main types of ritual?

14. What are the three stages in a rite of passage, according to Van Gennep?

15. Why are rites of intensification performed?

16. Distinguish between the two fundamental principles of magic.

17. In what ways does Navajo witchcraft reflect Navajo social structure?

18. How are witch hunts used for societal control?

19. What is the role of witchcraft among the Navajo?

20. What are the psychological functions of religion?

21. What are the social functions of religion?

22. How and why do revitalization movements emerge?

Fill-in-the-Blank

1. A society's _____ is the collective body of ideas that members of a culture generally share concerning the ultimate shape and substance of their reality.

2. A hallmark of religion is belief in _____.

3. In the nineteenth century European thinkers believed that _____ would eventually eclipse religion.

4. The set of gods and goddesses in a society are called its _____.

5. In most societies with subsistence bases in _____ or _____, deities are conceptualized as masculine.

6. A belief that nature is animated by spirits is called _____.

7. A concept of impersonal power, such as mana, is called _____.

8. _____ are specialists who have acquired spiritual power, which they can use on behalf of human clients.

9. _____ was a pioneer in the study of rites of passage.

10. When Mende girls are initiated into adult society, they undergo _____.

11. A ceremony to bring rain to a drought-stricken community is a _____.

12. The three stages of a life crisis ritual are _____, _____, and _____.

13. _____ wrote *The Golden Bough*.

14. _____ magic is based on the assumption that things that are similar to each other have an effect on each other.

15. Assuming that a person's fingernail clippings, hair, blood, and so on retain a spiritual connection to that person is the basis for _____ magic.

16. Among the Navajo, _____ is a way of expression and channeling hostile feelings.

17. A _____ is a social movement whose intent is to totally transform a society.

Multiple-Choice Practice Questions

1. Islamic fundamentalism in Iran and Christian fundamentalism in the United States demonstrate that _____.
   a. science has succeeded in destroying religion in the twentieth century
   b. religious activity is prominent in the lives of social elites.
   c. science meets basic needs
   d. religion is a powerful and dynamic force in society today
   e. science is wrong

2. _____ may be defined as the beliefs and patterns of behavior by which people try to control those aspects of the universe that are otherwise beyond their control.
   a. Political organization
   b. Government
   c. Kinship
   d. Common-interest associations
   e. Religion

3. Which of the following is **least** likely to be extensively involved in religious beliefs and activities?
   a. single women with ten children living below the poverty line, who dropped out of school at age fourteen
   b. members of food-foraging societies with limited scientific knowledge
   c. peasants in a feudal society
   d. members of lower classes in an urban-industrial society
   e. wealthy members of urban-industrial societies with advanced scientific knowledge

4. A people's collection of gods and goddesses is called a _____.
   a. mana
   b. shaman
   c. pantheon
   d. priest
   e. fetish

5. Belief in a supreme being who controls the universe is usually associated with _____.
   a. bands
   b. tribes
   c. chiefdoms
   d. states
   e. multinational corporations

6. If religious belief reflects the structure of society, in which types of society would you expect to find widespread belief in ancestral spirits?
   a. those in which descent groups play a major role in social organization
   b. those with a disproportionately large number of old people
   c. those with a disproportionately large number of young people
   d. those in which neolocal marital residence are the rule
   e. those with egocentric systems such as the kindred

7. The belief that nature is animated with spirits is called _____.
   a. animation
   b. anima
   c. animatism
   d. animism
   e. ennui

8. A _____ is a full-time religious specialist who occupies an office that has a certain rank and function.
   a. shaman
   b. priest
   c. witch
   d. magician
   e. diviner

9. In acting as a healer, the shaman _____.
   a. accurately diagnoses medical problems
   b. may improve the patient's state of mind, which aids in recovery

c. may be coping with his or her own problems by becoming intensely involved with the problems of others

d. provides reassurance to the community through an elaborate drama that may involve trickery

e. "may improve the patient's state of mind, which aids in recovery," "may be coping with his or her own problems by becoming intensely involved with the problems of others," and "provides reassurance to the community through an elaborate drama that may involve trickery"

10. Ceremonies such as bar mitzvah, elaborate wedding ceremonies, baby showers, and graduation parties that help individuals make major changes in their lives are referred to as rites of _____.

    a. transition
    b. intensification
    c. separation
    d. passage
    e. incorporation

11. A funeral ceremony may be regarded as _____.

    a. a rite of passage
    b. an opportunity to restore the equilibrium of the group
    c. an opportunity for individuals to express their feelings in a structured way that ensures continuation of society
    d. a rite of intensification
    e. "a rite of passage," "an opportunity to restore the equilibrium of the group," "an opportunity for individuals to express their feelings in a structured way that ensures continuation of society," and "a rite of intensification"

12. In *The Golden Bough,* _____ distinguished between religion and magic.

    a. Bronislaw Malinowski
    b. Franz Boas
    c. Sir James Frazer
    d. Sir Edward Tylor
    e. Clifford Geertz

13. Many magical incantations require the use of fingernail clippings of the intended victim. This is an example of _____.

    a. imitative magic
    b. contagious magic
    c. witch magic
    d. nightmare magic
    e. scientific thinking

14. Magic involves the manipulation of powers for good or evil, whereas witchcraft involves the possession of an innate power used for _____.
    a. religious purposes
    b. scientific reasons
    c. malevolent or benevolent purposes
    d. traditional societies
    e. societies that lack religion

15. Religion, magic, and witchcraft are all **similar** in which of the following ways?
    a. They all disappear once modern education and scientific training expand.
    b. They all share the common goal of improving social relationships within a community.
    c. They are all associated with morose nonconformists who try to destroy society.
    d. They provide explanations of events and are mechanisms of social control.
    e. They are all morally neutral.

16. A belief in _____ enables people to explain why things go wrong by blaming certain individuals who are said to have the internal psychic ability to cause harm to others.
    a. witchcraft
    b. magic
    c. divination
    d. contagion
    e. evil

17. Which of the following illustrate the psychological functions of religion?
    a. among the Holy Ghost People of the United States, handling snakes and drinking strychnine is a common feature of their worship; one explanation of this behavior is that by confronting the possibility of death, they achieve a sense of awe and transcendence
    b. an Islamic judge who orders the hand of a thief cut off can sleep soundly at night because he thinks of himself as merely the agent of divinely inspired justice
    c. the Navajo Indian origin myth provides every Navajo with a sense of this place in an orderly universe
    d. a person raised in the Catholic religion feels tremendous guilt when she/he commits a wrong
    e. "among the Holy Ghost People of the United States, handling snakes and drinking strychnine is a common feature of their worship; one explanation of this behavior is that by confronting the possibility of death, they achieve a sense of awe and transcendence," "an Islamic judge who orders the hand of a thief cut off can sleep soundly at night because he thinks of himself as merely the agent of divinely inspired justice," and "the Navajo Indian origin myth provides every Navajo with a sense of this place in an orderly universe"

18. A _____ is a deliberate effort by members of a society to construct a more satisfying culture.
    a. divination
    b. rite of intensification
    c. fetish

    d. lineage system

    e. revitalization movement

19. Which of the following statements about revitalization movements is **incorrect**?

    a. The purpose of revitalization movements is to reform society.

    b. Revitalization movements always fail because they require too much change to be tolerated.

    c. All known major religions, including Judaism, Christianity, and Islam, began as revitalization movements.

    d. Revitalization movements may be completely unrealistic.

    e. Revitalization movements may be adaptive and give rise to long-lasting religions.

20. N/um generally remains dormant in a healer until an effort is made to activate it. Among the ways to activate n/um are _____.

    a. trance dance

    b. hallucinogenic drugs

    c. medicinal curing ceremony

    d. solo singing

    e. trance dance, medicinal curing ceremony and solo singing

21. In southern Africa's Swaziland all types of illnesses are generally thought to be caused by _____ or _____.

    a. viruses/bacteria

    b. negative karma/negative attitude

    c. sorcery/loss of ancestral protection

    d. poor hygiene/poverty

    e. none of these

22. Which of the following have the Swazi **not** traditionally relied upon for treatment of disease?

    a. herbalists

    b. diviner mediums

    c. Christian faith healers

    d. general practitioners

    e. they rely on all of these; herbalists, diviner mediums, Christian faith healers and general practitioners

23. In a country where there is one traditional healer for every 110 people, but only one physician for every 10,000, the potential benefit of cooperation between physicians and healers seems self-evident. However, it was unrecognized until proposed by anthropologist _____.

    a. Edward C. Green

    b. Harald Prins

    c. Sir Edward B. Tylor

    d. William L. Ury

    e. R. R. Marett

24. Religion is viewed most simply as organized belief in the _____, and all fulfill numerous social and psychological needs.
    a. Christianity
    b. social system
    c. supernatural
    d. prevailing culture
    e. magic

25. _____ is considered a nature-oriented religion.
    a. Wicca
    b. Reform Judaism
    c. New Catholicism
    d. Seventh Day Adventist
    e. Atheism

26. In addition to so-called "New Age" enthusiasts, faith healers and many other evangelists among fundamentalist Christians share most of the characteristics of _____.
    a. Buddhism
    b. Shintoism
    c. Taoism
    d. shamanism
    e. socialism

27. The meanings ascribed to sensations experienced in altered states and made of their content are _____ determined; hence local traditions always vary in their detail.
    a. politically
    b. economically
    c. biologically
    d. culturally
    e. hallucinagenically

28. Which of the following mountains is the scene of a sacred pilgrimage for the Hindus and Buddhists in Tibet?
    a. Mt. Kailash
    b. Mt. McKinley
    c. Mt. Aconcagua
    d. Springer Mountain
    e. Mt. Everest

29. Anthropologist _____ defined religion as "a set of rituals, rationalized by myth, which mobilizes supernatural powers for the purpose of achieving or preventing transformations of state in man and nature."
    a. E. E. Evans-Pritchard
    b. E. Adamson Hoebel

c. Hilda Kuper

d. A. R. Radcliffe-Brown

e. Anthony F. C. Wallace

30. The _____ Indians maintained that each person had a personal spirit that could detach itself and travel about apart from the body, while the latter remained inert.

    a. Cayuga

    b. Hopi

    c. Cheyenne

    d. Penobscot

    e. Mayan

31. In the United States millions of people have learned something about shamans through reading _____ accounts of his experiences with Don Juan, the Yaqui Indian shaman.

    a. R. R. Marett's

    b. Carlos Castaneda's

    c. Edward B. Tylor's

    d. Laura Nader's

    e. Colin Turnbull's

32. The rites of passage that help individuals through the crucial crisis of their lives can be divided into three stages. Which of the following would be those stages?

    a. separation

    b. transition

    c. incorporation

    d. acquisition

    e. separation, transition and incorporation

33. Widely known among American Indians are the _____, who possess a detailed concept of witchcraft.

    a. Algonkian

    b. Cree

    c. Gros Ventre

    d. Navajo

    e. Shoshone

34. In the United States, _____ is an example of a revitalization movement that is enormously successful in gaining acceptance in the wider society.

    a. the Unification Church

    b. Mormonism

    c. the Branch Davidian

    d. the Heaven's Gate cult

    e. Jonestown

35. _____ forms part of a cultural system's superstructure, which comprises a society's worldview.
    a. Political philosophy
    b. Economic organization
    c. Social structure
    d. Religion
    e. The arts

36. Followers of _____ in the U.S. today number 1.28 million.
    a. Islam
    b. Buddhism
    c. Hinduism
    d. Judaism
    e. Wicca

37. Which of the following is considered a nature-oriented religion and has 310,000 adherents today?
    a. Lutheran
    b. Buddhism
    c. Shintoism
    d. Wicca
    e. Holy Rollers

True/False Practice Questions

1. The belief that nature is animated by spirits is called animism.
   True or False

2. Rituals reinforce social solidarity and thus enable individuals and groups to get through crisis.
   True or False

3. Rites of intensification help individuals get through a crisis.
   True or False

4. Religion provides an orderly model of the universe and reduces fear and anxiety.
   True or False

5. Interceding with the spirits and drawing out their invisible arrows is the task of (Ju/'hoansi) healers.
   True or False

6. Among the Ju/'hoansi only men can possess the powerful healing force called *n/um*.
   True or False

7. *N/um* is the Ju/'hoansi equivalent of *mana*.
   True or False

8. The trances that healers go into are considered harmless; they simply lose consciousness.
   True or False

9. The power of healers' n/um is all that is thought to protect the healer in a trance from actual death.
   True or False

10. Today biomedical germ theory is universally accepted in societies around the world.
    True or False

11. Religion is viewed most simply as organized belief in the supernatural that does not fulfill any social and psychological needs.
    True or False

12. Science, with its creation of new technologies, has helped diminish religious practice in the United States.
    True or False

13. Faith healers and many other evangelists among fundamentalist Christians have nothing in common with shamanism.
    True or False

14. The meanings ascribed to sensations experienced in altered states and made of their content are culturally determined.
    True or False

15. In fact, the custom of clitoridectomy is practiced by some in New York State.
    True or False

16. Far from causing the death of religion, the growth of scientific knowledge, by producing new anxieties and raising new questions about human existence, may have contributed to the continuing practice of religion in modern life.
    True or False

17. Religion is a part of all known cultures.
    True or False

18. The patriarchal nature of Western society is expressed in its theology.
    True or False

19. Shamanism is absent in modern industrial societies like the United States.
    True or False

20. In an attempt to deal with problems that defy ordinary explanation or solutions through material means, people appeal to, or seek influence and even manipulate spiritual or supernatural beings and powers.
    True or False

21. As pointed out in the textbook, people often turn to religion in the hope of reaching a specific goal, such as the healing of physical, emotional, or social ills.
    True or False

Practice Matching

Match the culture with its characteristic.

1. _____ Navajo
2. _____ Burma
3. _____ Ibibio
4. _____ Sioux
5. _____ Mende

a. West African people who practice female initiation rite involving clitoridectomy.

b. Southwestern Native Americans with a witchcraft tradition.

c. Native Americans of the plains who started the Ghost Dance as a religious revitalization.

d. a culture where a rejected lover may request the aid of a sorcerer

e. Sub-Saharan African people with a witchcraft tradition.

Short Answer

1. Discuss the relationship between worldview and religion.

2. Is there a difference between religion and spirituality? If so, what is it?

3. What is the anthropological definition of the term "shaman"?

4. What are rites of intensification? Provide examples.

5. What are rites of passage? Explain each of the stages.

6. Compare and contrast priests and shamans.

7. What is magic? Provide examples.

8. What are revitalization movements? How do they contribute to society?

9. Define witchcraft.

10. What are ancestral spirits?

Practice Essays

1. Bronislaw Malinowski, in his classic essay *Magic, Science, and Religion,* claimed that each of these was a viable mode of cognition and that most societies exhibit all of them in variable proportions. In what ways does magical thinking persist in contemporary North America? Is it likely to persist into the future?

2. Identify and describe the various ways the Jo/'hoansi activate the powerful healing force called n/um.

3. How is modern medicine reconciled with traditional beliefs in Swaziland?

4. What is shamanism and how can the widespread occurrence of shamanism be explained?

5. Religious rituals are religion in action. Describe what in fact is accomplished by religious rituals.

6. What is a revitalization movement? Explain how and why do they come into existence?

Solutions

Fill-in-the-Blank

1. worldview
2. supernatural beings
3. science
4. pantheon
5. pastoralism, intensive agriculture
6. animism
7. animatism
8. Shaman
9. Arnold Van Gennep
10. clitoridectomy
11. rite of intensification
12. separation, transition, incorporation
13. Sir James George Frazer
14. Imitative
15. contagious
16. witchcraft
17. revitalization movement

Multiple-Choice Practice Questions

1. D
2. E
3. E
4. C
5. D
6. A
7. D
8. B
9. E
10. D
11. E
12. C
13. B
14. C
15. D
16. A
17. E
18. E
19. B
20. E
21. C
22. D
23. A
24. C
25. A
26. D
27. D
28. A
29. E
30. D
31. B
32. E
33. D
34. B
35. D
36. C
37. D

True/False Practice Questions

1. T
2. T
3. F
4. T
5. T
6. F
7. T
8. F
9. T
10. F
11. F
12. F
13. F
14. T
15. T
16. T
17. T
18. T
19. F
20. T
21. T

Practice Matching

1. B
2. D
3. E
4. C
5. A

Chapter 14

The Arts

Synopsis

Challenge Issues: What is art? Why do anthropologists study art? What are the functions of art? This chapter examines the ethnocentric assumptions implicit in most Western definitions of the arts and artists. It distinguishes different types of creative activity, such as the visual and verbal arts and music and attempts to come up with a cross-culturally valid definition of art. The chapter concludes with a discussion of the impact of globalization of art.

Chapter Objectives

   I.   the anthropological study of art

  II.   visual art

 III.   verbal art

 IV.   musical art

  V.   functions of art

 VI.   art, globalization, and cultural survival

Key Terms

art	legend
epic	motif
ethnomusicology	myth
folklore	tale
iconic images	tonality

Exercises

The Anthropology Resource Center (ARC)

The Anthropology Resource Center is a dynamic, subfield-specific website that provides a wealth of materials for both students and instructors to reinforce key concepts in anthropology. All of the resources and activities encourage students to apply anthropology beyond the textbook and classroom. ARC can be reached through the weblink http://thomsonedu.com/. After selecting the discipline of "Anthropology" under "Humanities and Social Sciences," go directly to ARC for a wide range of resources that bring anthropology to life through pictures, interviews, news items, interactive displays, maps, and more. (This site is passcode-protected for both instructors and students.)

Review Questions

1. Distinguish between secular and religious art.

2. What are the basic kinds of verbal arts studied by anthropologists?

3. Give an example of how myth expresses the world view of a people.

4. Distinguish between legend and myth.

5. Who was Federica de Laguna and what were her contributions to anthropology?

6. What role does poetry play in the lives of the Bedouins?

7. What type of society is likely to have epics? Why?

8. What aspects of legends are of interest to anthropologists?

9. Why are anthropologists interested in tales?

10. What are the functions of music?

11. Distinguish between art and craft.

12. What is the importance of entopic phenomena?

13. How has globalization affected art?

14. Are there any universal characteristics of art?

15. Why do marketing experts routinely employ music and pictorial images in their advertising?

Fill-in-the-Blank

1. The term "verbal arts" is preferred to the term _____, a term developed in the nineteenth century to refer to traditional oral stories of European peasants.
2. The word "myth," in _____ usage, refers to something that is widely believed to be true but is not.
3. Tabaldak and Odziozo are characters in the origin myth of the _____.
4. Legends are _____ narratives that recount the deeds of heroes, the movements of people, and the establishment of customs.
5. Studies of tales in the southeast United States now indicate that they originated in _____ rather than Europe.
6. "Little songs" that occur every day were studied among the _____.
7. The study of music in its cultural setting is called _____.
8. The term _____ is used to refer to scale systems and their modifications in music.
9. An alternative to the Western octave system is the _____, which is defined by five equidistant tones.
10. Two people playing different patterns of beats at the same time is called _____.
11. The cultures of _____ have a particularly rich tradition of sculpture.
12. The Peyote Cult is found among the _____ Indians in Mexico.
13. The human nervous system produces images out of which patterns are construed. These are called _____.

Multiple-Choice Practice Questions

1. Whether useful or non-useful, all art is an expression of _____.
   a. the innate need to be impractical
   b. a fundamental human capacity for religious expression
   c. state-level societies that can afford specialists
   d. political domination of minorities by elites
   e. the symbolic representation of form and the expression of feeling that constitutes creativity

2. The observation that all cultures include activities that provide aesthetic pleasure suggests that
_____.
    a. humans may have an innate or acquired need to produce art
    b. the human mind requires the stimulation of imaginative play to prevent boredom
    c. all societies, from food-foraging bands to industrial states, include art in their culture
    d. art is a necessary activity in which all normal, active members of society participate
    e. "humans may have an innate or acquired need to produce art," "the human mind requires the stimulation of imaginative play to prevent boredom," "all societies, from food-foraging bands to industrial states, include art in their culture," and "art is a necessary activity in which all normal, active members of society participate"

3. Anthropologists prefer to use the term *verbal arts* rather than the term *folklore* because the term _____.
    a. *folklore* is used only by linguists; the term *verbal arts* is used only by anthropologists
    b. *verbal arts* sounds more sophisticated
    c. *verbal arts* is more scientific
    d. *folklore* implies lack of sophistication and is a condescending term to use
    e. *folklore* refers only to fairy tales

4. The type of verbal arts that has received the most study and attention is _____.
    a. poetry
    b. incantations
    c. narratives
    d. proverbs
    e. riddles

5. In the myth of Tabaldak and Odziozo, Tabaldak first created the Abenakis from stone and then from living wood. What does this tell us about the functions of myth?
    a. Myths function to tell actual history; the Abenakis believe that they were originally made of wood.
    b. Myths bring humor into the lives of the Abenakis because the myths are so ridiculous.
    c. Myths function primarily to provide entertainment; the Abenakis know they were not made from wood, but like to tell this story to visiting anthropologists who are so gullible.
    d. Myths function to express a culture's world view; the Abenakis see themselves as belonging to the world of living things rather than to the nonliving world of stone.
    e. Myths provide skills of woodworking and stone masonry to the Abenakis.

6. Because legends contain details of a people's past, they are a form of history; because they often give a picture of a people's view of the world and humanity's place in it, they are like _____.
    a. poetry
    b. religion

c. magic

d. kinship systems

e. myths

7. When an anthropologist uses the term _____, he or she is referring to a category of verbal narratives that are secular, non-historical, and seen primarily as a source of entertainment.

   a. "folklore"

   b. "myth"

   c. "tale"

   d. "legend"

   e. "drama"

8. Your text describes a type of narrative found in many cultures in which a peasant father and his son, while traveling with their beast of burden, meet a number of people who criticize them. What is the motif?

   a. The "motif" refers to the psychological motives of the characters in a story, in this case the desire of the son to do better than his father.

   b. "Motif" means the historical background to the story, in this case the history of exploitation of the peasantry.

   c. The "motif" refers to the story situation, in this case a father and son trying to please everyone.

   d. "Motif" means the physical environment in which the story occurs, in this case the yam gardens of Ghana.

   e. The "motif" refers to the economic background, in this case feudalism.

9. The "little songs" of the Bedouin are considered un-Islamic; they are the discourse of children, used to express rebellious ideas and feelings. Thus they are _____.

   a. anti-structural

   b. forbidden

   c. sung among Europeans only

   d. sung only when the Bedouins are away from their homeland

   e. sung only at marriages

10. The field of ethnomusicology _____.

   a. is concerned with human music rather than natural music

   b. is the study of music in its cultural setting

   c. began in the nineteenth century with the collection of folk songs

   d. concerns the organization of melody, rhythm, and form in a culture's music

   e. "is concerned with human music rather than natural music," "is the study of music in its cultural setting," "began in the nineteenth century with the collection of folk songs," and "concerns the organization of melody, rhythm, and form in a culture's music"

11. Scale systems and their modifications in music are called _____.
    a. tonality
    b. ethnomusicology
    c. sculpture
    d. verbal arts
    e. pentatonic

12. During the Washington Peace March in the sixties, thousands of people sang the song "We Shall Overcome." This song expressed a feeling of common purpose to counteract repression and to reform society. It created a sense of unity among diverse members of the crowd. This example illustrates the _____ of music.
    a. social functions
    b. geographical distribution
    c. tonality
    d. mythological features
    e. polyrhythms

13. Objects that are trivial, low in symbolic content, or impermanent are usually considered products of _____.
    a. an ethnomusicologist
    b. a tale
    c. craft
    d. art
    e. sculpture

14. The Huichol Indians use _____ in order to induce trance for artistic and religious purposes.
    a. cocaine
    b. peyote
    c. poppies
    d. heroin
    e. none of the above

15. _____ worked with the Tlingit Indians in order to help trace their cultural roots.
    a. Bronislaw Malinowski
    b. Franz Boas
    c. Federica de Laguna
    d. Meyer Fortes
    e. Margaret Mead

16. Verbal arts include _____.
    a. narratives
    b. dramas
    c. proverbs

    d. riddles

    e. all of the above

17. Laboratory research shows that humans typically move through _____ stages during a trance.

    a. 2

    b. 4

    c. 1

    d. 3

    e. 9

18. In the United States numerous examples exist of marginalized social and ethnic groups attempting to gain a larger audience and more compassion for their plight through song. Perhaps no better example exists than _____.

    a. Mexican Americans

    b. Chinese Americans

    c. Native Americans

    d. Puerto Ricans

    e. African Americans

19. A surprisingly large number of _____ in European and African tales are traceable to ancient sources in India.

    a. stories

    b. myths

    c. motifs

    d. devices

    e. lines

20. Which of the following music forms emerged out of the African American experience in the United States?

    a. opera

    b. polka

    c. ranchera

    d. waltz

    e. jazz

21. What do White performers like Elvis Presley and Pat Boone have in common?

    a. They were not influenced by African American music.

    b. They wrote their own music.

    c. They wrote their own lyrics.

    d. They presented their own versions of African American music to Black audiences.

    e. They presented their own versions of African American music to White audiences.

22. Perhaps the oldest form of artistic expression is _____.
    a. oil painting
    b. sculpting
    c. pottery
    d. body decoration
    e. cave drawings

23. A true _____ is basically religious, in that it provides a rationale for religious beliefs and practices.
    a. folktale
    b. legend
    c. myth
    d. epic tale
    e. riddle

24. Much of what passes for history, consists of the _____ we develop to make ourselves feel better about who we are.
    a. poems
    b. parables
    c. legends
    d. ballads
    e. fictions

25. A surprisingly large number of motifs in European and African tales are traceable to ancient sources in _____.
    a. China
    b. Japan
    c. Latin America
    d. India
    e. Mesopotamia

26. Applying the interpretive approach to southern African rock art requires knowledge of which two subjects?
    a. Mbuti ethnography
    b. Bushman ethnography
    c. nature of the rain forest
    d. nature of the trance
    e. Bushman ethnography and nature of the trance

27. _____ serves as a powerful way for a social or ethnic group to assert its distinctive identity.
    a. Tale
    b. Music

c. Chant

d. Poem

e. Play

28. Art can affirm group solidarity and identity beyond kinship lines as evidenced by the United States' _____.

    a. turkey

    b. crescent moon

    c. cedar tree

    d. maple leaf

    e. bald eagle

29. The cedar tree is _____'s symbol of group solidarity and identity.

    a. Canada

    b. Italy

    c. Jordan

    d. Lebanon

    e. Syria

30. Tattoos in the U.S. have traveled a long way from the tattoo of old: brought to North America by way of _____'s 18th century of the Pacific.

    a. Christopher Columbus

    b. Sir Francis Drake

    c. Captain James Cook

    d. Ferdinand Magellan

    e. Juan Cabrillo

True/False Practice Questions

1. The term "tale" refers to a type of narrative that is secular, non-historical, and seen primarily as a source of entertainment.
   True or False

2. Legends are semi-historical narratives which recount the deeds of heroes, the movement of peoples and the establishment of local customs.
   True or False

3. The word "myth," in popular usage, refers to something that is widely believed to be true but probably is not.
   True or False

4. Legends provide clues as to what is considered appropriate behavior in a culture.
   True or False

5. Bushman rock images are banal, meaningless artifacts akin to urban graffiti in the U.S.
   True or False

6. Bushman art has a single, one-to-one 'meaning' that it unequivocally transmits from the maker to the viewer.
   True or False

7. Bushman rock art were simply records of religious experiences.
   True or False

8. Bushman rock art were not just pictures, but rather powerful things in themselves that could facilitate the mediation of the cosmological realms.
   True or False

9. Bushman rock art were just pictures that had no power to effect changes in the shamans' states of consciousness.
   True or False

10. The making of art was, for the Bushman, an idle pastime.
    True or False

11. For centuries shamans had fought in the spiritual realm with marauding shamans of illness, so, their art suggests, did they battle in the spiritual realm with the colonists.
    True or False

12. Bushman rock art itself and the belief system in which it was embedded is much more complex than was ever thought.
    True or False

13. As another organizing factor in music, whether regular or irregular, tonality may be more important than rhythm.
    True or False

14. The music of a marginalized group of former slaves eventually captivated the entire world, helping their descendants to escape their marginal status.
    True or False

15. In the United States, the arts often are seen as something of a frill, something to be engaged in for personal enjoyment apart from more productive pursuits or to provide pleasure for others, or both.
    True or False

16. A true myth is basically religious in that it provides a rationale for religious beliefs and practices.
    True or False

17. For the most part, legends and myths are the products solely of nonliterate, non-industrialized societies.
    True or False

18. An art form that has developed recently is tattooing. It involves the puncturing and coloring of human skin with symbolic designs.
    True or False

19. Almost anything humans can lay their hands on can become an object of artistic expression- skin, hair, dress, dwellings, vehicles, weapons, utensils, etc.
    True or False

20. Some form of visual art is a part of every historically known human culture.
    True or False

21. Music is of little importance in the cultural preservation and revitalization efforts of indigenous peoples.
    True or False

Short Answer

1. As a type of symbolic expression, visual art may be representational or abstract. Discuss these two categories of visual art.

2. Describe the functional purposes of tattooing.

3. Explain the process by which tattooing has expanded in the U.S. from a working-class folk art into a more widespread and often refined aesthetic practice.

4. What meaning do tattoos have for middle-class North Americans?

5. Distinguish between visual and verbal art.

6. Who was Federica de Laguna and why was she important to anthropology?

7. What is folklore?

8. What is ethnomusicology?

9. Compare and contrast legend and epic.

10. What is peyote and how do the Huichol Indians use it?

Practice Essays

1. Many famous biographies or novels about artists in the West stress the individual creativity of the artist (for example, James Joyce's *Portrait of the Artist as a Young Man*). Artists are portrayed as people who have the vision to rise above and beyond the social and cultural conditions into which they were born, sometimes even crossing the boundaries of normality as typically defined by society. How is this vision of the artist different from the conception of artists held by non-Western societies?

2. Discuss art's general meaning. What is art's role in Bushman communities?

3. Bushman rock art extends beyond the generation of religious experience to the negotiation of political power. Demonstrate why this is so.

4. Discuss why it is important to protect the cultural heritages of tribal peoples. Why is it of concern to anthropologists?

5. Discuss the influence the African American experience has had on American music.

6. What are the social functions of music? Provide examples.

7. Art in all its forms has countless functions beyond providing aesthetic pleasure. Discuss some of the functions of art.

8. Art can and does play a role in indigenous rights efforts. Explain art's role i indigenous people's efforts to gain their rights.

Solutions

Fill-in-the-Blank

1. folklore
2. popular
3. Abenaki
4. psuedo-historical
5. West Africa
6. Bedouins
7. ethnomusicolgy
8. tonality
9. pentatonic system
10. polyrythm
11. America's Northwest coast
12. Huichol
13. entopic phenomena

Multiple-Choice Practice Questions

1. E
2. E
3. D
4. C
5. D
6. E
7. C
8. C
9. A
10. E
11. A
12. A
13. C
14. B
15. C
16. E
17. D
18. E
19. C
20. E
21. E
22. D
23. C
24. C
25. D
26. E
27. B
28. E
29. D
30. C

True/False Practice Questions

1. T
2. T
3. T
4. T
5. F
6. F
7. F
8. T
9. F
10. F
11. T
12. T
13. F
14. F
15. T
16. T
17. F
18. F
19. T
20. T
21. F

Chapter 15

Processes of Change

Synopsis

Challenge Issues: Why do cultures change? How do cultures change? What is modernization? This chapter discusses the mechanisms of cultural change and examines anthropology's role in the changes sweeping the world. The use of the term modernization is considered from a cross-cultural perspective. The chapter concludes with an evaluation of the concept of globalization, a form of accelerated modernization that creates benefits and challenges to human society.

Chapter Objectives

I.   mechanisms of change

II.   repressive change

III.   reactions to repressive change

IV.   rebellion and revolution

V.   modernization

Key Terms

acculturation
cultural loss
diffusion
ethnocide
genocide
modernization

primary innovation
rebellion
revolution
secondary innovation
syncretism
tradition

Exercises

The Anthropology Resource Center (ARC)

The Anthropology Resource Center is a dynamic, subfield-specific website that provides a wealth of materials for both students and instructors to reinforce key concepts in anthropology. All of the resources and activities encourage students to apply anthropology beyond the textbook and classroom. ARC can be reached through the weblink http://thomsonedu.com/. After selecting the discipline of "Anthropology" under "Humanities and Social Sciences," go directly to ARC for a wide range of resources that bring anthropology to life through pictures, interviews, news items, interactive displays, maps, and more. (This site is passcode-protected for both instructors and students.)

Review Questions

1. Distinguish between primary and secondary innovation.

2. Provide an example of primary innovation.

3. Why is it that cultural context provides the means for innovation to occur?

4. What things have European Americans borrowed from American Indians?

5. What is meant by cultural loss?

6. Describe the nature of acculturation.

7. What factors seem to be underlying causes of genocide?

8. What does the field of applied anthropology attempt to accomplish?

9. How did the Trobriand Islanders react to the British game of cricket?

10. What is the purpose of revitalization movements?

11. What are the precipitators of rebellion and revolution?

12. What is the problem with the term "modernization"?

13. What are the four sub-processes of modernization?

14. What is meant by the "culture of discontent"?

Fill-in-the-Blank

1. Innovations based on the chance discovery of some new principle are called _____ innovations, while innovations resulting from the deliberate application of these principles are called _____ innovations.

2. The spread of customs or practices from one culture to another is called _____.

3. According to Ralph Linton, as much as _____ percent of a culture's content is due to borrowing.

4. _____ occurs when groups with different cultures come into intensive, firsthand contact and one or both groups experience massive cultural changes.

5. In the United States the switchover to the metric system is still less than _____ percent.

6. The extermination of one people by another is called _____.

7. The field of _____ anthropology uses anthropological knowledge and techniques for practical purposes.

8. The applied work of anthropologist _____ is helping to address problems along Senegal River in Africa.

9. Under conditions of acculturation, indigenous populations may blend foreign traits with those of their own culture to form a new cultural system. This response is called _____.

10. The Trobrianders blended indigenous traditions with the British game of _____.

11. _____ movements are deliberate attempts by members of a society to construct a more satisfactory culture.

12. A revitalization movement that attempts to bring back a destroyed but not forgotten way of life is called a _____ or revivalistic movement.

13. A revitalization movement that attempts to resurrect a suppressed, outcast group that has its own special subcultural ideology and has occupied an inferior social position for a long time is called _____.

14. Revolutions have occurred only during the last _____ years, since the emergence of centralized systems of political authority.

15. Modernization refers to the process of cultural and socioeconomic change whereby developing societies become more similar to _____ industrialized societies.

16. The _____ aspect of modernization means a shift in population from rural areas to cities.

17. The Skolt Lapps in the country of _____ traditionally supported themselves by fishing and reindeer herding.

18. The Shuar Indians promoted cooperative _____ ranching as their new economic base.

19. Hundreds of millions of people in our world struggle against _____.

20. With modernization, _____ find themselves in an increasingly inferior postion worldwide.

Multiple-Choice Practice Questions

1. In New England, the culture of English speakers replaced the various cultures of Native Americans living along the coast. Your text says that this occurred because _____.
   a. English-speaking culture was superior to Native American culture
   b. Native American culture was superior to English-speaking culture
   c. it is inevitable that English speakers will replace other cultures that they encounter
   d. a combination of accidental factors contributed to the success of English speakers in establishing colonies along coastal New England
   e. the success of English speakers was only a temporary setback for the progressive development of Native American culture

2. The chance discovery of some new principle that can be applied in a variety of ways is called _____.
   a. primary innovation
   b. primary syncretism
   c. applied anthropology
   d. millenarism
   e. diffusion

3. The deliberate use of basic ideas in some practical application, such as making use of the knowledge of how electricity works to develop the telephone, is called _____.
   a. revitalization
   b. millenarism
   c. modernization
   d. integrative mechanism
   e. secondary innovation

4. Copernicus's discovery that the earth orbits the sun rather than vice versa _____.
   a. was a primary innovation that met the cultural goals and needs of his time
   b. was a primary innovation that was out of step with the needs, values, and goals of the time
   c. was a secondary innovation that put into application the discovery by Ptolemy that heavenly bodies moved on crystalline spheres around the earth
   d. was a secondary innovation that was deliberately developed by Copernicus to destroy the Polish Church
   e. resulted from diffusion of ideas from India

5. According to the North American anthropologist Ralph Linton, about 90 percent of any culture's content comes from _____.
   a. primary innovation
   b. diffusion
   c. invention
   d. syncretism
   e. revolution

6. In biblical times, chariots and carts were widespread in the Middle East, but by the sixth century the roads had deteriorated so much that wheeled vehicles were replaced by camels. This illustrates that cultural change is sometimes due to _____.
   a. primary invention
   b. secondary invention
   c. diffusion
   d. revitalization
   e. cultural loss

7. As a result of prolonged firsthand contact between societies A and B, which of the following might happen?
   a. Society A might wipe out society B, with it becoming a new dominant society.
   b. Society A might retain its distinctive culture but lose its autonomy and come to survive as a subculture such as a caste or ethnic group.
   c. Society A might be wiped out by society B, with only a few scattered refugees living as members of the dominant society.
   d. The cultures of A and B might fuse, becoming a single culture with elements of both.
   e. "Society A might retain its distinctive culture but lose its autonomy and come to survive as a subculture such as a caste or ethnic group," "Society A might be wiped out by society B, with only a few scattered refugees living as members of the dominant society," and "The cultures of A and B might fuse, becoming a single culture with elements of both"

8. The extermination of one group of people by another, often deliberately and in the name of progress, is called _____.
   a. genocide
   b. acculturation
   c. diffusion
   d. applied anthropology
   e. primary innovation

9. The field of applied anthropology developed _____.
   a. through efforts to help the poor in North American society
   b. in sociology classrooms
   c. in industry
   d. in colonial situations
   e. through the efforts of women opposed to prohibition

10. In acculturation, subordinate groups will often incorporate new cultural elements into their own culture, creating a blend of old and new; a reinterpretation of new cultural elements to fit them with already existing traditions is called _____.

    a. syncretism

    b. innovation

    c. diffusion

    d. integrative mechanism

    e. modernization

11. A deliberate attempt by members of society to construct a more satisfying culture may be called _____.

    a. a secondary innovation

    b. a revitalization movement

    c. an enervating movement

    d. syncretism

    e. a primary innovation

12. Which of the following is/are considered to be important precipitators of rebellion and revolution?

    a. a sudden reversal of recent economic advances

    b. the media no longer support the government

    c. the established leadership loses prestige

    d. a strong, charismatic leader organizes attacks on the existing government

    e. "A sudden reversal of recent economic advances," "The media no longer support the government," "The established leadership loses prestige," and "A strong, charismatic leader organizes attacks on the existing government"

13. The term "modernization" _____.

    a. is a relativistic rather than ethnocentric concept

    b. refers to the process of cultural and socioeconomic change whereby societies acquire the characteristics of industrialized societies

    c. refers to a global and all-encompassing process whereby modern cities gradually deteriorate

    d. can be used to show that all societies go through the same stages of evolutionary development, culminating in the urban-industrial state

    e. is not used by anthropologists

14. As modernization occurs, which of the following changes are likely to follow?

    a. literacy increases

    b. religion decreases

    c. kinship plays a less significant role

    d. social mobility increases

    e. literacy increases, religion decreases, kinship plays a less significant role and social mobility increases

15. The division of a single role (which serves several functions) into two or more roles (each with a single specialized function) is called _____.
    a. millenarization
    b. modernization
    c. structural differentiation
    d. industrialization
    e. diffusion

16. Changes in Skolt Lapp society occurred because _____.
    a. men switched from reindeer herding to other sources of income
    b. the number of reindeer declined
    c. snowmobiles were used to herd reindeer
    d. society became hierarchical
    e. women became more powerful than men

17. Carol Jenkins works in _____ researching the emergence of new diseases.
    a. Samoa
    b. Mexico
    c. Canada
    d. Papua New Guinea
    e. Australia

18. IDA stands for _____.
    a. Internal Development Service
    b. International Development Anthropology
    c. Institute for Development Association
    d. Institute for Development Anthropology
    e. Institute for Developing Anthropology

19. _____ plants and herbs used by Native Americans for medicinal purposes have at one time or another been included in official government-approved prescription and over-the-counter drugs.
    a. 50
    b. 150
    c. 200
    d. 240
    e. 350

20. The most common pattern characterizing violence against indigenous people in Brazil is _____.
    a. racism
    b. impunity (guilty party gets away with crime)
    c. massacres

d. illegal detention

e. police brutality

21. When people are able to keep faith with their traditions in the face of powerful outside domination, the result is _____.

a. depression

b. assimilation

c. cretinism

d. gratification

e. syncretism

22. Over his career of 35 years of scholarly and applied work, _____, has made pioneering contributions to the development of applied anthropology and to anthropology's role in public policy and service.

a. R. J. Gordon

b. Michael M. Horowitz

c. Pierre Van Den Berghe

d. George Augustus Robinson

e. August Dvorak

23. Horowitz's tireless dedication has been critical in institutionalizing anthropology as an applied science in international development organizations like which of the following?

a. Nasdaq

b. the World Bank

c. USAID

d. the Food and Agriculture Organization (FAO)

e. the World Bank, USAID and the Food and Agriculture Organization (FAO)

24. The ultimate source of all change is _____.

a. religion

b. war

c. innovation

d. the weather

e. biological

25. _____ occurs when there is a spread of certain ideas, customs or practices from one culture to another.

a. acculturation

b. innovation

c. revolution

d. syncretism

e. diffusion

26. In 1637 a deliberate attempt was made to destroy the Pequot Indians by setting fire to their village at Mystic, Connecticut and then shooting down all those who sought to escape being burned alive. This is considered an act of _____.

    a. attrition

    b. contrition

    c. absolution

    d. genocide

    e. fratricide

27. _____ has contributed greatly to our understanding of ethic in anthropological research and the phenomenon of peasantry worldwide.

    a. Robert Lowie

    b. Napoleon Chagnon

    c. Walter Goldschmidt

    d. E. Adamson Hoebel

    e. Eric Wolf

28. _____ movements that attempt to revive traditional ways of the past are not restricted to "underdeveloped" countries; in the U.S., the Reverend Pat Robertson is a leader in such a movement.

    a. New Age

    b. Mystical

    c. Revitalization

    d. Nostalgic

    e. Revolutionary

29. The process of modernization can be best understood as consisting of several subprocesses. Which of the following are subprocesses of modernization?

    a. extraterrestrial development

    b. technological development

    c. agricultural development

    d. weapons development

    e. technological development and agricultural development

30. The discovery of fired clay by migratory food foragers occurred _____ years ago.

    a. 5,000

    b. 15,000

    c. 25,000

    d. 30,000

    e. 45,000

31. The gap between the rich and poor people of the world is widening rather than narrowing. This has led to the development of what anthropologist Paul Magnarella has called a new

    _____.

a. "culture of poverty"

b. "culture of unrealized dreams"

c. "culture of unrealistic expectations"

d. "culture of discontent"

e. "class of have nots"

32. _____ is the massive change that comes about with the sort of intensive, firsthand contact that occurs when dominant societies forcefully expand their activities beyond their borders, leading less powerful societies to abandon their traditional cultures in favor of the foreign.

a. Assimilation

b. Integration

c. Acculturation

d. Adaptation

e. Accommodation

33. The English crossed the Atlantic Ocean equipped with the political and military techniques for dominating other peoples; in addition they came with the ideology of _____, which they believed justified the dispossessing of America's indigenous peoples.

a. democracy

b. socialism

c. communism

d. a just war

e. Christianity

34. It was not until some time between _____ and _____ years ago that people recognized a highly practical application of fired clay and began using it to make pottery containers and cooking vessels.

a. 9000 and 8500

b. 15,000 and 10,000

c. 30,000 and 25,000

d. 7500 and 6000

e. 3000 and 2500

35. The worldwide process of accelerated modernization in which all parts of the earth are becoming interconnected in one vast interrelated and all-encompassing system is known as _____.

a. revolution

b. rebellion

c. acculturation

d. globalization

e. capitalism

36. One of the first and most prominent anthropologists to focus on worldwide transformations was _____.

    a. Franz Boas

    b. Eric Wolf

    c. Laura Nader

    d. Ralph Nader

    e. John Swetnam

True/False Practice

1. Death rates among indigenous peoples in the New World reached 75 to 90 percent after colonization.
   True or False

2. Genocide is a recurring problem
   True or False

3. Brazil's indigenous peoples have shown that they are unable to resist or adapt to demands imposed upon them from outside.
   True or False

4. Trobrianders resisted the imposition of cricket by the British.
   True or False

5. Today there is an increasing rate of worldwide poverty.
   True or False

6. The impact of Michael M. Horowitz's applied anthropological research has been by all standards minimal.
   True or False

7. Acts of genocide are a fairly recent phenomena.
   True or False

8. Each revitalization movement that has occurred in the United States has been unique and different from the other.
   True or False

9. By their very nature, all revolts are revolutionary in their consequences.
   True or False

10. Your text has made it clear that genocide is always a deliberate act.
    True or False

11. Because stability is a striking feature of many cultures like the food foragers, subsistence farmers, and pastoralists these cultures are changeless.
    True or False

12. Frequently, rather than just adding new things to those already in existence, the acceptance of a new innovation leads to the loss of an older one.
    True or False

13. Genocide is not always a deliberate act.
    True or False

14. Progress, like adaptation, is a consequence rather than a cause of change.
    True or False

15. Wheeled vehicles virtually disappeared from Morocco to Afghanistan about 1500 years ago. They were replaced by camels because of a reversion to the past by the region's inhabitants.
    True or False

16. The practical application of anthropology is thriving today as never before.
    True or False

Practice Matching

Match the culture with its characteristic.

1. _____ Skolt Lapps
2. _____ Shuar
3. _____ Trobrianders
4. _____ Maya
5. _____ Yanomami

a. a group in Central America that does not support the use of chemical fertilizers
b. a group which adapted a British form of sport to their own cultural needs
c. Native Americans of Ecuador who formed a federation to protect their interests.
d. Arctic Scandinavians whose society was radically changed by snowmobiles.
e. Brazilian group that suffered ethnocide

Short Answer

1. What is applied anthropology?

2. Explain why the Taliban movement in Afghanistan was considered a revitalization movement.

3. Why has it been suggested that it would be impossible for most peoples of the world to achieve something resembling a middle-class standard of living comparable to that of many people in the Western world in the near future?

4. What are mechanisms of change?

5. What are the steps involved in modernization?

6. What is the difference between ethnocide and genocide?

7. What is the difference between revolution and rebellion?

8. Define culture loss. Provide an example.

8. Why is change essential to cultural survival?

9. What is the role of globalization in culture change?

10. Define innovation and provide examples of each.

Practice Essays

1. Describe the impact of modernization on Skolt Lapps and Shuar Indians.

2. In what ways can the rising tide of Islamic fundamentalism in the Middle East and other areas of the world be seen as a revitalization movement? Are there other terms from the chapter that could apply to this phenomenon? What might anthropology contribute to our understanding of such movements?

3. The violence that occurred on Indian Day in Brazil 1997 brought to the surface old problems and wounds that have never healed. Identify and discuss these old problems and wounds that still exist in Brazilian society.

4. What is the role of anthropology in the study of new diseases?

5. Explain why revolution is a relatively recent phenomenon.

6. Discuss the contributions of Michael M. Horowitz to the development of applied anthropology and to anthropology's role in public policy and service.

7. Reactions of indigenous peoples to changes forced upon them vary considerably. Describe how various groups have reacted to forced change.

8. Belief in "progress" and its inevitability has important implications for North Americans as well as others. What are some implications? Explain.

9. Explain the difference between a rebellion and a revolution. Provide recent examples of both.

Solutions

Fill-in-the-Blank

1. primary, secondary
2. diffusion
3. 90
4. Acculturation
5. 50
6. genocide
7. applied
8. Michael Horowitz
9. syncretism
10. cricket
11. Revitalization
12. revolutionary
13. revolutionary
14. 5,000
15. Western
16. urbanization
17. Finland
18. cattle
19. poverty
20. women

Multiple-Choice Practice Questions

1. D
2. A
3. E
4. B
5. B
6. E
7. E
8. A
9. D
10. A
11. B
12. E
13. B
14. E
15. C
16. C
17. D
18. D
19. C
20. B
21. E
22. B
23. E
24. C
25. E
26. D
27. E
28. C
29. E
30. C
31. D
32. C
33. D
34. A
35. D
36. B

True/False Practice

1. T
2. T
3. F
4. F
5. T
6. F
7. F
8. F
9. F
10. F
11. F
12. T
13. T
14. T
15. F
16. T

Practice Matching

1. D
2. C
3. B
4. A
5. E

Chapter 16

Global Challenges, Local Responses, and the Role of Anthropology

Synopsis

Challenge Issues: What can anthropologists tell us of the future? What are the cultural trends in our globalizing world? What problems must be solved for humans to have a viable future? In this concluding chapter the text considers the role of anthropological knowledge in facing the world of the future. The ability to systematically consider cultural facts and their underlying structures is an anthropological specialty that provides a basis for solving problems engendered by the three primary cultural trends – globalization, ethnic and religious resurgence of distinctive cultural identities, and a growing concern that rising populations, spiraling energy use, and expanding energy consumption are devastating our environment.

Chapter Objectives

    I.   the cultural future of humanity

    II.   structural power in the age of globalization

    III.   problems of structural violence

Key Terms

hard power

multiculturalism

replacement reproduction

soft power

structural power

structural violence

Exercises

The Anthropology Resource Center (ARC)

The Anthropology Resource Center is a dynamic, subfield-specific website that provides a wealth of materials for both students and instructors to reinforce key concepts in anthropology. All of the resources and activities encourage students to apply anthropology beyond the textbook and classroom. ARC can be reached through the weblink http://thomsonedu.com/. After selecting the discipline of "Anthropology" under "Humanities and Social Sciences," go directly to ARC for a wide range of resources that bring anthropology to life through pictures, interviews, news items, interactive displays, maps, and more. (This site is passcode-protected for both instructors and students.)

Review Questions

1. What shortcomings are evident in future-oriented literature?

2. What makes anthropologists uniquely suited to contribute to planning for the future?

3. Can the world today be described as a global culture?

4. Why are predictions of a politically integrated world probably incorrect?

5. Give an example of how misunderstandings might actually increase in a global culture.

6. Give some contemporary examples of ethnic resurgence.

7. How does the concept of ethnocentrism interfere with cultural pluralism?

8. Provide examples of structural violence.

9. What is thought to be the immediate cause of world hunger? Provide examples.

10. Why is the suggestion that countries adopt agricultural practices similar to the United States not necessarily sound advice?

11. What is meant by culture of discontent?

Fill-in-the-Blank

1. Anthropologists try to be _____, meaning they take into account many interacting factors to understand the functioning of the complex whole.

2. External migration in search of better conditions and opportunities is called _____.

3. Indigenous people represent _____ percent of the world's population.

4. _____ is an official policy that asserts the values of different cultures co-existing within a country.

5. There are about _____ recognized states in the world today, but an estimated 5,000 national groups.

6. An important force for global unity are the _____ corporations that cut across national boundaries.

7. The major problem associated with cultural pluralism is _____.

8. _____ power organizes and orchestrates the systematic interaction with and among societies.

9. A great deal of the violence in the world is not due to the unique and personal decisions of individuals but to social, political, and economic conditions; this is referred to as _____ violence.

10. The population of the world today is about _____.

11. Coercive power that is backed up by economic and military force is _____, while _____ is co-optive.

12. _____ is a fluid and shifting landscape of migrants, refugees and other moving groups.

13. In total, some _____ people in the world are undernourished.

14. Replacement reproduction refers to a rate of reproduction in which a couple has no more than _____ children.

Multiple-Choice Practice Questions

1. Most people plan for the future by looking at trends in _____.
   a. ancient history
   b. hemlines
   c. third-world countries
   d. food supplies
   e. recent history

2. Anthropologists are trained to develop effective predictions of the future because they are _____.
   a. aware of cultural relativity
   b. good at seeing how parts fit together into a large whole
   c. trained to have an evolutionary perspective

    d. able to see short-term trends in long-term perspective

    e. "aware of cultural relativity," "good at seeing how parts fit together into a large whole," "trained to have an evolutionary perspective," and "able to see short-term trends in long-term perspective"

3. Over the past five thousand years, political units have _____.

    a. grown steadily smaller in size

    b. grown steadily larger in size and fewer in number

    c. eliminated multinational corporations

    d. promoted individual freedoms

    e. eliminated slavery

4. Multinational corporations _____.

    a. have been widespread in Western culture since medieval times

    b. were very common during the colonial period

    c. have become a major force in the world today since the 1950s

    d. have been disintegrating since the 1950s

    e. promote relativistic rather than ethnocentric ideas

5. Which of the following expresses the **negative** consequences of multinational corporations on the international and domestic scenes?

    a. Multinational corporations cross-cut nations and thus achieve a global unity.

    b. Multinational corporations have become a major force in the world since the 1950s.

    c. Multinational corporations have become so powerful that they have been able to influence government decisions so that they benefit the company rather than the people.

    d. Multinational corporations are products of the technological revolution.

    e. They have developed sophisticated data-processing techniques that enable them to keep track of worldwide operations.

6. Cultural pluralism _____.

    a. may constitute a temporary stage in a process of integration into a single melting-pot culture

    b. implies the absence of bigotry and racism

    c. implies respect for the cultural traditions of other peoples

    d. may result from conquest or from several culturally distinct groups occupying an area that eventually becomes unified as a larger political entity

    e. "may constitute a temporary stage in a process of integration into a single melting-pot culture," "implies the absence of bigotry and racism," "implies respect for the cultural traditions of other peoples," and "may result from conquest or from several culturally distinct groups occupying an area that eventually becomes unified as a larger political entity"

7. Which of the following represent the **negative** consequences of ethnocentrism?

    a. By believing that another culture is inferior to yours, you can, with a sense of righteousness, destroy its temples, cottage industry, polygynous practices, and so on in order to bring it into line with your culture's standards of appropriate behavior and belief.

    b. Ethnocentrism confers a sense of pride in and loyalty to one's own cultural traditions.

    c. Ethnocentrism provides a feeling of psychological gratification that one is living the right kind of life.

    d. Ethnocentrism contributes to a sense of personal worth.

    e. Ethnocentrism strengthens social solidarity.

8. _____ is violence produced by social, political, and economic structures rather than by the unique and personal decisions of individuals.

    a. Torture

    b. Modernization

    c. Structural violence

    d. Insanity

    e. Religion

9. The change from subsistence farming to cash crops _____.

    a. enables farmers to enlarge their holdings and feed their families more effectively

    b. results in the relocation of subsistence farmers to urban areas or to lands ecologically unfit for farming

    c. leads to the decline of multinational corporations

    d. supports cultural pluralism

    e. leads to revitalization

10. The main reason an Asian wet-rice farmer might choose not to adopt North American techniques of intensive agriculture is because _____.

    a. he or she cannot afford to buy the chemical products typically used in this type of agriculture

    b. the North American method requires at least eight calories of energy to be expended for every calorie produced, whereas the wet-rice farmer produces three hundred calories for every calorie he or she invests

    c. the North American method produces toxic substances that destroy delicate ecological balances

    d. he or she predicts that the North American method, while successful for a short period of time, is sowing the seeds of its own destruction

    e. "he or she cannot afford to buy the chemical products typically used in this type of agriculture," "the North American method requires at least eight calories of energy to be expended for every calorie produced, whereas the wet-rice farmer produces three hundred calories for every calorie he or she invests," "the North American method produces toxic substances that destroy delicate ecological balances," and "he or she predicts that the North American method, while successful for a short period of time, is sowing the seeds of its own destruction"

11. Pollution, although a worldwide consequence of certain agricultural and industrial activities, is more of a problem in _____ because chemicals that may be banned in richer nations can be used more easily.
    a. poor countries
    b. industrialized countries
    c. arctic countries
    d. Mediterranean countries
    e. ocean areas

12. If a country achieves "replacement reproduction," this means that _____.
    a. people produce only enough children to replace themselves when they die
    b. each reproductive couple has no more children
    c. its population will immediately stop growing
    d. its population will continue to grow for another fifty years
    e. every other generation can have children

13. The most extreme form of female genital mutilation.
    a. female circumcision
    b. breast implantation
    c. infibulation
    d. appendectomy
    e. tonsillectomy

14. The most dramatic illustrations of the tendency for states to come apart recently would be which of the following?
    a. the breakup of the Soviet Union
    b. the breakup of Yugoslavia
    c. the separation of East Timor from Indonesia
    d. the separation of Vietnam into North and South Vietnam
    e. the breakup of the Soviet Union, the breakup of Yugoslavia and the separation of East Timor from Indonesia

15. The dramatic revival of pastoral nomadism in Mongolia would be an example of _____.
    a. cultural pluralism
    b. cultural decline
    c. nationalistic pride
    d. ethnic backwardness
    e. ethnic resurgence

16. The Universal Declaration of Human Rights was officially adopted by all members of the United Nations in _____.
    a. 1964
    b. 1948
    c. 1973
    d. 2000
    e. 2001

17. The immediate cause of world hunger has more to do with which of the following?
    a. food production
    b. food distribution
    c. food storage
    d. warfare
    e. food distribution and warfare

18. The world's population is projected to peak in 2050 at about _____ billion people.
    a. 20
    b. 7.5
    c. 9.37
    d. 8.35
    e. 5.23

19. Which of the following would make the anthropologist well-equipped to make valid projections about the world's future?
    a. their holistic perspective
    b. their evolutionary perspective
    c. their 100 years of cross-cultural research
    d. their familiarity with alternative ways to deal with a wide variety of problems
    e. "their holistic perspective," "their evolutionary perspective," "their 100 years of cross-cultural research," and "their familiarity with alternative ways to deal with a wide variety of problems"

20. Which of the following groups of women experience body mutilation as part of engendering rites?
    a. North American
    b. Sudanese
    c. Filipino
    d. Mexican
    e. North American and Sudanese

21. After a 10-year intensive study of relations between producers and consumers of products and services, anthropologist _____ found repeated and documented offenses by business that cannot be handled by present complaint mechanisms, either in or out of court.

    a. Margaret Mead

    b. Laura Nader

    c. Ruth Benedict

    d. Linda Coco

    e. Howard Zinn

22. Approximately how many languages are there today in the world?

    a. 54

    b. 2,700

    c. 6,000

    d. 8,500

    e. 100

23. The problem with _____ is that it all too easily can be taken as a charter for manipulating other cultures for the benefit of one's own, even though this does not have to be the choice.

    a. ethnocentrism

    b. ambivalence

    c. provincialism

    d. prejudice

    e. narrow-mindedness

24. Which of the following are reasons impoverished people tend to have so many children?

    a. Children are their main resource.

    b. Children provide a needed labor pool to work farms.

    c. Children are the only source of security for the elderly.

    d. Infant mortality rates are unusually high in impoverished areas.

    e. "Children are their main resource," "children provide a needed labor pool to work farms," "children are the only source of security for the elderly," and "infant mortality rates are unusually high in impoverished areas."

25. In order to solve the problems brought about by global structural violence it has been suggested that dramatic changes in cultural values and motivations, as well as social institutions, will be required. Which of the following would have to change to help solve the problems due to structural violence?

    a. the emphasis on individual self-interest

    b. uncontrolled materialism

    c. a sense of social responsibility

    d. excessive consumption

    e. "the emphasis on individual self-interest," "uncontrolled materialism," and "excessive consumption."

26. However humanity changes biologically, _____ remains the chief means by which humans try to solve their problems.

    a. technology

    b. religion

    c. faith in humankind

    d. military might

    e. culture

27. Since _____ seems unstoppable, we are compelled to ask: How can the thousands of different cultures, developed in the course of centuries if not millennia, deal successfully with the multiple challenges hurled at them?

    a. assimilation

    b. acculturation

    c. global warming

    d. globalization

    e. industrialization

28. This vast, mountainous country is inhabited by several major ethnic groups, including the Pashtun who live mainly in the south, and Tajik, Uzbek, Hazara, and Turkmen who live mainly in the north. The country being described is _____.

    a. Turkey

    b. Iraq

    c. Uzbekistan

    d. Chechnya

    e. Afghanistan

29. The Karen people's separatist movement is taking place in Myammar, formerly known as _____.

    a. Turkey

    b. Burma

    c. Croatia

    d. India

    e. Indonesia

30. Although, of late, there has been a tendency for political units to fragment into smaller ones, there are instances of reunification. Best known is the 1990 reunification of _____.

    a. Ireland

    b. Germany

    c. Czechoslovakia

    d. Korea

    e. Indonesia

31. In 1992 a Maya woman named _____ won the prestigious Nobel Peace Prize for her tireless work on behalf of indigenous rights.
    a. Eva Balam-Ek
    b. Luisa Che
    c. Raquel Maria Casas
    d. Rigoberta Menchu
    e. Maria Elena Ujpan

32. During the 20th century, more than _____ million people died from human-made famine.
    a. 44
    b. 63
    c. 12
    d. 21
    e. 100

True/False Practice Questions

1. Multinational corporations have constituted a strong force for global unity.
   True or False

2. Structural violence refers to violence produced by social, political, and economic structures rather than by the unique and personal decisions of individuals.
   True or False

3. The change from subsistence farming to cash crops leads to economic improvements in countries that made the change.
   True or False

4. There is less structural violence today than there was 100 years ago.
   True or False

5. The question of choice is central to the story of how medicine and business generate controlling processes in the shaping of women's bodies.
   True or False

6. Sudanese and other African women, North American women, and others experience body mutilation as part of engendering rites.
   True or False

7. The American Society of Plastic and Reconstructive Surgery operates like a commercial enterprise instead of a medical society. They saturate the media to sell women breast implants. The author of the original study, Linda Coco, refers to this idea as "patriarchal capitalism."
   True or False

8. Social surveys indicate that, to the extent that women internalize the social imperative that they can enhance their lives by enhancing their breasts, they feel they are making the decision on their own.
   True or False

9. There are an estimated 192 national groups today in 5,000 different states.
   True or False

10. Today, about 10 million people are internally displaced or have crossed international borders as refugees.
    True or False

11. Indigenous people represent less than 1 percent of the world´s total population.
    True or False

12. During the 1970s the world´s indigenous peoples began to organize self-determination movements.
    True or False

13. The international community recognizes the concept of group rights.
    True or False

14. Sweden has a GDP that exceeds Wal-Mart.
    True or False

15. ExxonMobil has a GDP that exceeds that of Saudi Arabia.
    True or False

16. The immediate cause of world hunger has less to do with warfare than with food production and food distribution.
    True or False

17. Multinationals are extremely new phenomena on the global scene, appearing first around the 1950s.
    True or False

18. According to the original study "Standardizing the Body," the question of choice is central to the story of how medicine and business generate controlling processes in the shaping of women's bodies.
    True or False

19. In so-called "underdeveloped" countries, women have become a source of cheap labor for large corporations, as subsistence farming has given way to mechanized farming.
    True or False

20. It seems the more divergent cultural traditions are, the easier it is to make pluralism work.
    True or False

21. Though a minority of the world's population, people in the developed countries consume the most resources and generate the bulk of hazardous wastes.
    True or False

22. Hard power is co-optive.
    True or False

23. The more divergent cultural traditions are, the more difficult it seems to make pluralism work.
    True or False

24. Today there is a growing culture of discontent.
    True or False

25. Today there are more underfed people in the world than overfed people.
    True or False

26. Not all people who are overweight or obese are so because they eat too much junk food and have too little exercise.
    True or False

Short Answer Practice Questions

1. In 1991 the Soviet Union broke-up into numerous independent republics. Identify those newly minted independent states.

2. The tendency for multi-ethnic states to splinter can be seen in separatist movements that arise. Identify the separatist movements that have arisen recently in various countries.

3. What is multiculturalism?

4. Why can it be said that global corporations are products of the technology revolution?

5. Define structural power.

6. Some dramatic changes in cultural values and motivations, as well as in social institutions, are required if humans are going to realize a sustainable future for generations to come. What changes in cultural values and motivations need to occur?

Practice Essays

1. What contributions can anthropology make in our globalizing world?

2. One of the most heated debates arising from the public health concern over breast implants is whether the recipient's decision is voluntary or whether control is disguised as free will. Explain what is meant by this.

3. What are the greatest challenges in resolving the exploitations associated with structural violence?

4. Despite a worldwide trend toward "Westernization," and despite the pressure for traditional cultures to disappear, it is clear that cultural differences are still very much with us in the world today. In fact, a tendency for peoples globally to resist modernization, and in some cases retreat from it, is strengthening. Explain ethnic resurgence, using examples.

5. Discuss the rise of multinational corporations and their impact on the domestic as well as the international scene.

6. Debate the pros and cons of a global culture.

7. Identify and discuss the problems of structural violence.

8. Solving the problems of the global society depends on, among other things, lessening the gap between the living standards of the impoverished and developed countries. How might this be accomplished?

9. Explain how global corporations might be a force for worldwide political integration.

10. Discuss examples of structural power and structural violence that you have observed within your own community? How might such issues best be addressed within a civil society?

11. There are two major interacting forces in the worldwide arena "hard power" and "soft power." Define these two types of power and discuss how they interact. Provide examples.

12. A key factor in the world's food crisis is a dramatic rise in the world's population. Discuss population growth worldwide.

13. There are actually two "cultures of discontent." One exists in poor countries and the other is emerging in wealthy countries. Discuss each of the "cultures of discontent" and describe how they came about.

Solutions

Fill-in-the-Blank

1. holistic
2. voluntary migration
3. 5
4. multiculturalism
5. 192
6. multinational
7. ethnocentrism
8. structural
9. structural
10. 6–7 billion
11. hard power, soft power
12. Ethnoscapes
13. 1 billion
14. two

Multiple-Choice Practice Questions

1. E
2. E
3. B
4. C
5. C
6. E
7. A
8. C
9. B
10. A
11. A
12. A
13. C
14. E
15. E
16. B
17. E
18. C
19. E
20. E
21. B
22. C
23. A
24. E
25. E
26. E
27. D
28. E
29. B
30. B
31. D
32. A

True/False Practice Questions

1. T
2. T
3. F
4. F
5. T
6. T
7. T
8. T
9. F
10. F
11. F
12. T
13. T
14. T
15. T
16. F
17. F
18. T
19. T
20. F
21. T
22. F
23. T
24. T
25. F
26. T